Andrew Banks and Geoff Morgan both have formidable reputations as specialists in senior sales, marketing, general management, and search and recruitment. They established Morgan & Banks in 1985. The group now has offices throughout Australia, New Zealand, Asia, Europe and North America. Their range of services include executive selection and search; psychological consulting; management consulting; management contracting; human resources consulting; training and development; and outplacement.

GW00382212

Morgan & Banks

Geoff Morgan & Andrew Banks

Getting That Job

How to
establish and
manage your
career into the
next millenium

Harper*Business*
An imprint of HarperCollins*Publishers*

To our parents, who gave us the capacity and the mission
to fulfil our ambitions

GEOFF AND ANDREW

Harper*Business*
An Imprint of HarperCollins*Publishers*, Australia

First published in Australia in 1999
Reprinted in 1999, 2000
by HarperCollins*Publishers* Pty Limited
ACN 009 913 517
A member of the HarperCollins*Publishers* (Australia) Pty Limited Group
http://www.harpercollins.com.au

Copyright © Geoff Morgan 1999

HarperCollins*Publishers*
25 Ryde Road, Pymble, Sydney, NSW 2073, Australia
31 View Road, Glenfield, Auckland 10, New Zealand
77-85 Fulham Palace Road, London W6 8JB, United Kingdom
Hazelton Lanes, 55 Avenue Road, Suite 2900, Toronto, Ontario M5R 3L2
and 1995 Markham Road, Scarborough, Ontario M1B 5M8, Canada
10 East 53rd Street, New York NY 10022, USA

National Library of Australia Cataloguing-in-Publication data:

Morgan, Geoff.
   The Morgan & Banks guide to getting that job.
   ISBN 0 7322 6626 2.
   1. Job hunting. 2. Career development. I. Banks. Andrew.
   II. Morgan & Banks Ltd. III. Title.
650.14

Every effort has been made to trace and acknowledge copyright holder/s of the cover
photograph. The publisher would be pleased to hear from copyright holder/s to rectify
the omission.

Printed in Australian by Griffin Press Pty Ltd on 79gsm Bulky Paperback

9 8 7 6 5 4 3
03 02 01 00

Acknowledgments

Morgan & Banks gratefully acknowledge a number of members of their staff who have contributed their expertise in the development of this book. The diagram of Projected Employment Growth by Occupation—1991–2001 was originally published in the Sydney Morning Herald.

CONTENTS

CONTENTS

STEP 2

STOCKTAKING YOUR ASSETS   25
Assessing your current position

STEP 3

CAPITALISING ON YOUR ASSETS   39
How to make the
most of what you've got

STEP 4
WHERE TO INVEST YOUR ASSETS   62
Researching the job market

STEP 5

STEP 8

MAKING YOUR JOB WORK FOR YOU   201
Developing your career

STEP 9

BEING YOUR OWN BOSS   218
Options and strategies

1. Options   219
   – executive contracting—a form of 'outsourcing'
   – turnaround management
   – management consultancy
   – projects and troubleshooting roles

2. Part-time and temporary work   229
   – part-time work
   – temporary work

3. Starting a small business—look before you leap   230

APPENDICES   235

INTRODUCTION

One of the great ironies of life is our capacity to make quantum leaps in some areas and no real headway in others. In the last 70 years we've walked on the moon, conquered Everest, created computers with artificial intelligence, discovered the Internet, and conceived sliced bread, velcro and nuclear fusion! Yet, in relative terms, we have made very little progress on how to match people to jobs which truly capitalise on their talents. The way employers identify people for work and the way people identify the right job and the right industry is still, in our opinion, highly inefficient.

Add to that *this fact*: most of us will seek new career opportunities at least five to seven times in a lifetime. No longer can one afford to wait passively on the sidelines for an opportunity to knock on your door. Indeed, when candidates indicate this is the first time in their career they have really had to search for a job, the statement is somewhat of an indictment: often they have failed to optimise their own peculiar skills, knowledge and career aspirations to get that job in which they *really excel*. There is no doubt that with the Internet, the ability for job-seekers and employers to find each other will improve dramatically.

However, Morgan & Banks has worked with employers for the last 15 years to assist them improve the clarity and efficiency with which to identify candidates with the appropriate skills, knowledge and attributes for a given task.

This book doesn't attempt to change the system—we *all* have to work together on that. However, we can help by sharing the distillation of many thousands of hours of interviews with both employers and candidates. *Getting that Job* is a tool to assist you improve your strike rate by optimising the way you identify your first or your next career, or contract role. In a competitive world it is no longer good enough to put a 'summary of your life' down on a few pieces of paper (a résumé or CV) and shoot it out into the marketplace haphazardly. Doing that is akin to saying: Here's my background, Employer, *you* work it out, and let me know if you have a job that suits!

In a rapidly shifting workplace you may have to rethink your future. It could lie in contracting, team management, outsourcing, working from home, running your own business, a consulting or entrepreneurial move, temping, job-sharing, retraining, or a complete career shift.

The twenty-first century is going to be all about *change*: and that means optimising and capitalising on our individual skills to gain maximum rewards—both material and non-material—in return for effort.

We hope this book will assist you in doing this job—the most important of your life—that much better.

GEOFF MORGAN & ANDREW BANKS

REASONS FOR CHANGE

Did you hear the one about the impact of technology on jobs in the twenty-first century?

Well, in the year 2005 (the story goes) a plane will be flown by a human being and a dog. It will be the human's job to feed the dog, and the dog's job to bite the human if he or she touches anything!

This boardroom parable highlights a concern that technology will continue to replace many of the functions that are currently performed by human beings. Now, one can fear these changes and become melancholic, or embrace the vast opportunities technology offers—as many employers are doing—and utilise them to share in improved productivity.

Back to our parable—only a cerebrally challenged canine would bite the hand that feeds it.

Theoretically, the use of information and technology will eventually lead to shorter working hours and new jobs will be created by the need to service a workforce with a higher expendable income and increased leisure time. Technology is already changing the way people are hired, and the skills and competencies they will need to meet the tasks of newly structured jobs in the future.

For most of us a good job is an important part of life, with 'good' being defined by individuals as to what suits them at this juncture in their life. We want the fulfilment of working in a position we enjoy, a position that allows suitable rewards and recognition, and from which we derive a great deal of enjoyment and satisfaction. Thus 'work' and 'life' are inextricable.

If work *is* an integral part of life, why do so many of us go to work simply to pay the rent? A recent international survey of over 1000 middle and senior management executives in Europe and North America found that four out of five of those surveyed felt that they were not in the ideal job with the ideal company. Four out of five probably sounds excessive, but what this figure really indicates is that individual expectations—in terms of salary, rewards, and what we want to actually do up to ten hours a day—are constantly changing. If you match that up against the changing needs of organisations in a competitive world, achieving a complete match is only a one in five shot!

Before you make a move, be sure the odds are in your favour. You might be better off staying put, gaining more experience to improve your chances in the stakes for *the ideal job*. Have you discussed your desire to move on to something different with your current employers? They might be able to accommodate your needs—if not immediately, then perhaps in the future.

However, if we assume that you have explored these options, there may still be various reasons why you might be dissatisfied with your present position and why you might contemplate a change.

- You feel there must be more to your career than your current role. Your enthusiasm has dissipated along with your energy levels to do that job.
- Inspired by some external event, you have made a conscious decision to go for a change of direction, industry or profession.
- You are ambitious and advancement in your current job is not coming as quickly as you'd like.
- Your decision has been made for you—you've been retrenched.
- You know you are in a dying industry and you're looking for an opportunity to translate your skills into a new growth area. Planning ahead!
- Perhaps you have been out of the workforce for a while, or you are a recent graduate who's never been in full-time employment, and you want to develop a strategy to get into the mainstream.

Before you can plan any move in terms of specific jobs or industries, you need to work out which job will be right for you in terms of the characteristics you consider important. This section gives you a formula for mapping this out.

WHAT HOLDS A PERSON IN A JOB?

What factors will encourage the contemporary employee to stay in an organisation?

Ideally they relate to personal achievement as well as the terms and conditions which offer real incentives. This is reflected in research results on factors which inspire an employee to stay in an organisation:

- reasonable security;
- interesting and fulfilling job content;
- adequate non-financial recognition;
- motivational leadership with a vision and clear direction;
- pay for performance that truly differentiates between levels of accomplishment—and, if possible, an incentive scheme that consistently provides additional rewards for high achievers;
- career planning by both employer and employee— enabling ongoing promotion and challenge;
- flexible remuneration packages—tailored to individual needs as much as possible;
- a 'learning' environment that offers ongoing training and real challenge, thus obtaining outstanding performances from ordinary people.

REASONS WHY YOU MIGHT STAY IN A JOB

The boiling frog

There is a well-known story about the boiling frog and it goes like this. If you take a pan of hot water and you throw in a live frog, it will jump quickly from the cauldron and hop safely away. But if you allow a frog to swim around in lukewarm water, gently heating the pan until it is boiling, the frog will not notice the slow but incremental change in the water temperature and it will remain there and die.

The biggest negative in a career can often be the Boiling Frog Syndrome: where you wake up ten years on and realise that you have missed the boat because you became so comfortable in your working environment you forgot to keep exploring your options. So beware of letting your career potential plateau and ultimately slip away—it's the soft option!

In the early part of the 1990s many people avoided radical career decisions because they felt, in the short term, it was more important to have a job. Career progression, more money, or some form of lifestyle change was put on hold as people looked more for security, stability of employment and, most importantly, continuity of employment.

People continue to avoid change because of the *fear factor*. Growing unemployment and large-scale retrenchments are a frightening feature of the last ten years as we cope with structural changes brought about by technology and changing world patterns of trade and demand. The early

1990s were about recession and recovery; but the main event was simply change! However, there is now a subtle shift occurring. New opportunities are emerging and people who deferred their expectations for career advancement are now re-entering the marketplace.

Of course, you could still find reasons (excuses?!) for postponing your career move:

- You remember what the job used to be like and you think it will pick up and get back to what it was. Don't fool yourself—forget about going back to your old job. It doesn't exist anymore.
- It may be convenient in some other way. It may enable you to do something else, achieve another goal outside your career: further education; starting a family—fine, but don't lose sight of your original goal.
- Security versus advancement. You are feeling comfortable and it's easy to rationalise why you're not ready to move: 'Maybe I should stay another year and do three or four more deals.' Admit it, you're thirty-three, working for a good institution, and you've been there nine years. It's time for a change—don't con yourself into not exploring options.
- You're worried your skills won't translate to another industry and you don't know your choices.
- Financial pressure. To make a career change, you know that, initially, you are going to have to step backwards in financial terms.
- Status quo. A change of company seems daunting. You're appreciated and known where you are; you will have to re-establish your credibility and make new client contacts and new friends.
- Loyalty is a wonderful quality in human beings. Your employers have been loyal to you, and you feel you owe it to them to stick around—that is a judgement that you

and only you can make. But loyalty is often used as a cop-out to take the pressure off actually having to contemplate a move and stretching yourself yet again in a new career—one where ultimately you can achieve your true potential in terms of job content, recognition, and income for you and your family.

We see many candidates who talk constantly about their fears of making a job move. Their new employer may not like them as much as their current employer. They may not do as well in the job as they hope they will. So many factors beyond their control could go wrong.

They completely overlook the risks of *not* moving, whereby—through a very gradual process—they become a kind of hostage, ultimately reaching a point where prospective employers are not interested in them anymore. Analyse *your* circumstances and motives and beware the boiling frog!

REASONS WHY PEOPLE LEAVE A COMPANY

An Australian corporation, agonising over 'the ones that got away', surveyed the motivations of those who left their company. They found in general:

- their job and career expectations were no more demanding on the surface than those of people who stayed with the company;
- lack of challenging opportunities and the company's lack of commitment to the individual played a critical role in the decision to leave;

- when their particular expectations were not met, they became dissatisfied and their commitment to the organisation waned;
- when they were dissatisfied they became susceptible to specific internal problems and were highly attracted to outside offers;
- there was usually one specific event that acted as the catalyst in their decision to leave—maybe just a bad day or a brief 'run in' with a colleague.

There were two other interesting findings from this survey. First, most of the employees who had left for 'greener pastures' had a positive view of their former company and nearly 75 per cent said they would have stayed had circumstances been different. And second, women were more likely than men to look for alternative positions within the company before deciding to make a career move to another organisation. Does that indicate women are more loyal than men, or just more pragmatic?

You'll note that remuneration was not even mentioned as a reason for searching for a new job. In most cases money is not the motivating force—it's usually because the organisation is not meeting other needs.

One of the most frequent comments in interviews with candidates looking to move on is that they feel the company's culture no longer suits them. This bears discussion, as it can often be a smokescreen for the real reasons that employees pursue other options.

Corporate culture is defined by one of the leading writers in the field, Edgar Schien, as the 'deeper level of basic assumptions and beliefs that are shared by members of an organisation, that operate subconsciously, and that define in a basic "taken-for-granted fashion" an organisation's view of itself and its environment'. What this really means is 'the way we do things around here', or how a company behaves collectively.

Culture isn't written into policy manuals, it's practised in meetings, carparks, customer contact points and an organisation's social gatherings.

An understanding of the cultural values of an organisation is essential in working out what makes a person fit into one organisation but not into another. High flyers in one culture may be barely able to exist in another, even if they possess all the right skills for the job.

Cultural variables which could contribute to dissatisfaction:

- The way a company administers its policies and procedures. Successful companies tend to have 'values'—a clearly identifiable 'code' of conduct which is flexible—rather than too many procedural manuals, rigidly applied.
- Supervision—one of the key variables here and the biggest clue as to how the company operates—is the way in which the management team gets the best out of people. The supervisory style should be flexible enough to manage the 'high competence, high motivation' individual, who operates with a high degree of autonomy, through to the 'low competence, low motivation' individual, who clearly needs to be directed.
- Quality of working conditions and the general environment.
- The way the salary package is put together; incentives or lack of them; and the flexibility of remuneration packaging.

You will need to consider the fact that you may move to a job that on *the surface* looks as if it's a smaller job because of the title (status), but when that job is analysed in terms of its content, its responsibility, its scope, and the new skills that you will acquire—it could well be a move ahead, or at least a transitional move which will subsequently take you in the right direction.

REASONS WHY
YOU MIGHT MOVE

In the 1980s, the major considerations for moving were:

- desire for more autonomy;
- lack of challenge;
- desire for more decision-making power;
- more remuneration;
- different job content;
- career at a natural end.

Let's look at some of these as relevant to now.

Desire for more autonomy—a benign form of ambition?

Way back in the 1970s, management guru Peter Drucker likened organisations of the future to an orchestra with the chief executive as the conductor. Although a large band of people reported to one individual, a strong beat of corporate values and guidelines kept the organisation harmoniously flowing in the same direction. In the case of the orchestra, of course, those values and guidelines are clearly noted in the music score.

It is not *just* information technology that has reduced the need for middle management. It is the way these organisations *use* technology to bypass whole layers of management, 'mainlining' information directly to those further down the ladder to achieve higher productivity and competitiveness. It's what tough customers used to call 'eliminating the middle man'.

In the 1980s, Total Quality Management (TQM) became a popular technology for improved efficiency in manufacturing. In the 1990s, TQM became less to do with shop-floor manufacturing and more to do with the desire for managements and their teams to work together. 'Behaviours' have actually changed and organisations have become receptive to these new processes.

By providing a framework of values (supported by training and development), companies can 'empower' more employees, thereby giving them greater autonomy. There is no longer the need for as much management around or above them, to furnish them with the information (or permission) to do their job well.

Empowerment is one of the new buzzwords: devolving decision-making to employees and allowing new channels to open so that employees can contribute to innovation and improved productivity. Technology has been the catalyst and the tool responsible.

These changes herald the emergence of the contemporary *knowledge worker*—a very mobile, competent, confident individual who continues to grow and learn and then transport those skills to whichever employer offers most in terms of future opportunity and remuneration. The knowledge worker will be attracted to an organisation that provides autonomy in the truest sense: where (once management has decided you have the *competencies* to do the job) you are left alone to work with minimal supervision and measured by advanced quantitative and qualitative systems which track inputs and outputs, rather than by someone (middle management) looking over your shoulder.

The concept of *competencies* focuses on what is expected of an employee in the workplace rather than on the learning process; it embodies the ability to transfer and apply skills and knowledge to new situations and environments. This is a broad concept of competency in that all aspects of work performance, and not only narrow skills, are included. It encompasses:

- the requirement to perform individual activities (task skills);
- the requirement to manage a number of different tasks within the job (task management skills);
- the requirement to respond to irregularities and breakdowns in routine (contingency management skills);
- the requirement to deal with the responsibilities and expectations of the work environment (job/role environment skills).

The competency-based approach to managing people is one of the most important recent developments. Unless it is factored into the recruitment process there will be a significant mismatch between recruiting this new knowledge worker and one who might be termed the more traditional employee who can't cope with a lack of direction.

We will come back to this when we get to the interview stage, focusing on the systems of this potential disparity.

Desire for greater remuneration

In today's more competitive world there have been two major changes. One is that organisations employ fewer people but pay the high achievers more. At the lower levels, however, where jobs can be more easily filled, salary structures have remained flat or, in some cases, gone backwards.

The other development is a move towards flexible salary packages. (*See* Step 7, Section 6 Salary Packages.)

There is no doubt that moving on to a bigger job in another company can accelerate an increase in remuneration. Clearly, however, there comes a point when too many moves are as bad as the Boiling Frog Syndrome mentioned earlier. You are seen to be job-hopping simply for the sake of a quick buck.

However, let us assume that you have had a few good years where you are, but as you just can't gain the desired quantum leap in remuneration you are motivated to explore other options.

People may make a vertical move for more money but they rarely take a role that is a lateral or sideways move. This job move might not necessarily take them up the corporate ladder or into an area which has more responsibility, but it might present an opportunity to learn new skills, provide more interest, and, because of that particular company's remuneration structure and incentive schemes, *also* provide a plus in terms of remuneration.

Watch for these types of jobs. They are another symptom of a rapidly changing employment environment: the shape and nature of jobs and companies means that spotting the real opportunities becomes more tricky—you have to think laterally!

As we will discuss later on, you can no longer judge a job by its title. You must look past the text in advertisements, or read between the lines in an employer's explanation, because what you may think *looks wrong* could be *right* and what *looks right* can sometimes be *quite wrong*.

Another change is the company car. This used to be a great status symbol, but with the move towards a total compensation cost-to-company package, it is now just becoming an integral part of the salary package. If you choose to drive a more expensive car, you will simply take less cash and vice versa.

Employers are more interested in productivity, the competencies of their workforce and monitoring *their* total cost of employment than worrying about what make of car you drive, whether your neighbours or peers approve of it, and how often you want to replace it with a new one.

In summary, a move towards better remuneration might cover:

- a more flexible package, one that suits your personal circumstances;
- a remuneration structure that doesn't give you any more up-front, but through incentives gives you the *capacity* to earn more based on performance;
- taking a new job as a transitional move where you can learn more skills and improve your remuneration;
- a straight upward move, where you take on more responsibility and satisfy your other requirements, as well as increase your income.

Career at a natural end

There are various reasons why you may have hit this spot:

- You're in a dying industry and there is a reduction in demand for the services and products you've been currently trained to provide.
- You have retired from your career at the required age (but you don't want to cease working).
- You're burnt out. You feel you have nothing more to offer the job and it no longer offers you satisfaction.
- You've been replaced by technology and need to embark on a new career to ensure employment.

So you need to change. You're at the end of a career but you're not ready to stop working. Your old job doesn't exist. Now is the time to think laterally about how you can translate your existing skills into a new arena. And you might have to think about retraining.

FALLACIES ABOUT CAREER PATHS

Fallacy: You can't move your career across industries. To get on you're better off staying with one company to develop your career potential rather than changing companies on a fairly regular basis.

Fact: Good people no longer think about a lifetime career with one company. Security and superannuation as reasons for moving or staying take second place to new challenges in the workplace. Unless your present employer has moved you around a great deal—and that means in quite different roles, not just geographical locations—by the time you reach thirty-five, many employers feel it is desirable for candidates to have had at least three jobs. You will have a broader base of experience than someone who has stayed in one organisation, and changing jobs gives you the opportunity to develop skills vital to career advancement in the future.

Fallacy: You can plan your lifetime career when you finish your initial training.

Fact: People don't necessarily know what they really want to do with their career when they have finished school or tertiary study. In fact, many people still don't know when they are in their thirties and considering a career change. The key is to optimise your interest and preferences against your skills to find the most challenging and remunerative job.

Fallacy: Previous experience is a prerequisite for getting into any industry.

Fact: In the last ten years there has been a rapid shift away from previous industry experience towards the calibre, quality and intellect of an individual. No longer do you need to have worked in a specific industry in order to be employed in a particular area. It's more a question of translating your skills as they relate to the position on offer. Employers are much more flexible these days—which, incidentally, is one of the reasons the door is open to more women to explore previously male-dominated industries than ever before.

About time!

Fallacy: A Master of Business Administration (MBA) degree will automatically get you a job.

Fact: Tertiary qualifications are very useful and clearly the relevant experience, a good personality, a positive attitude *and* an MBA will contribute to an outstanding career. But an MBA or higher tertiary qualification on its own is no passport to success. Educating and training should never cease but the qualification itself is less important than the fact you are demonstrating an ongoing thirst for knowledge. You are merely maintaining your relevance in today's world.

Fallacy: Women need to work harder than males to get to the same level in a corporation.

Fact: Women who are professional and businesslike, and achieve results, will get on in any organisation. It's important for women to recognise organisations that practise true equality and gravitate towards them. These organisations will be tougher to compete in than those with prejudices because they will have, by definition, a more flexible and talented workforce. Why? Because they are drawing from a larger pool of workers.

Fallacy: People with a public service background cannot get into private enterprise.

Fact: Sure, to some extent there has been a jaundiced view held by the private sector about public servants, and vice versa, but these days more and more public servants are leaving the security of the public sector (either voluntarily or involuntarily) and being hired by the private sector on the basis of their skills, knowledge and attributes.

Fallacy: Age is a barrier to changing a career.

Fact: Today people are looking more and more for people who can achieve the desired result, and if the person is forty-five to fifty-five, energetic, well presented and a professional, they are still a definite employment prospect. It works the other way too. If you are young, there is no reason to assume you won't be given a job with responsibility. What matters is what you can deliver. Many companies have managing directors who are in their early to mid thirties, and doing extremely well. Only inflexibility is a barrier to change.

Fallacy: You can plan your life and career path as soon as you graduate or finish your training. It will be plain sailing from there.

Fact: You can only have an effective five- to ten-year plan. Beyond that you are likely to be wasting your time because in a world changing so rapidly, if you try to make a longer-term plan, you lose the ability to be flexible and hold to a fixed path that, due to change, could lead nowhere.

Fallacy: Candidates who are currently working have a better chance of getting a job than those unemployed.

Fact: Human beings are strange. They often want something more, simply because someone else currently has that same thing. However, unemployment is a symptom of change, and smart employers recognise this. As long as you have a good employment history, the appropriate skills and a positive attitude, you stand an even chance. To capitalise on your advantages over the employed person (more time and no need for confidentiality), try to get on an outplacement program.

6 CIRCUMSTANCES BEYOND YOUR CONTROL

Okay, you've been fired, retrenched, or perhaps the company has gone bankrupt. Whatever—the circumstances are beyond your control.

You got yourself fired

If you have been fired, it is certainly a disadvantage but it does not make for an impossible situation. It's happened before and employers realise that circumstances change. There's a simple message—*make sure you understand the facts as they will be related to any new employer and plan your career search accordingly.*

Make sure you understand clearly how your references will be framed when you go for another job. *Make sure* that any job you apply for will deploy your strengths, not your weaknesses, unless of course you can prove that it was your employers who made a poor decision and not you! But the onus of proof is on you, not them, so be pragmatic.

Retrenchment

If your company doesn't exist anymore, or your job doesn't, then a decision has been made for you.

The first thing to realise is that *it's not the person who is redundant, it's the position,* and unfortunately you are the person in the position. You are not alone. It is not a personal slight. Retrenchment is something that may affect anyone and everyone.

You tend to hear the word 'redundancy' more than 'retrenchment' because this is what the Tax Office recognises.

For a redundancy to be bona fide and for an employee to reap all the possible rewards (like the termination payout being 95 per cent tax-free), it needs to be a management-initiated redundancy program.

So what are you going to do about it?

If you are on an outplacement program (an employer-assisted career transition course), you already have a distinct advantage because it is this systematic process, more than anything else, that will improve your chances of getting another job.

Part of handling retrenchment is getting mentally prepared to go on and find another job. Someone who is confident, articulate, and able to discuss openly and freely why they were retrenched, will find something somewhere else in due course.

Some people, retrenched lunchtime Wednesday, have approached a recruitment agency that afternoon. They want to start a job immediately. They'll take anything, it doesn't matter what the dollars are, what the role is. *Don't panic.* For the majority of people, retrenchment hasn't been the disaster they thought it would be. Many have actually started completely new careers, or gone on to bigger and better jobs.

Companies are not really interested in why you've been made redundant, because it is now universally recognised that this does not reflect on the person. They are only interested in whether you have the right skill sets (competencies) to match their criteria for the position, and whether they feel you fit into their organisation.

Use this time for reflection. There are positive benefits. You now have a unique opportunity to reassess where you are going with your career, with your life. What sort of role will you take on in the future? For instance, you might decide to work from home; spend more time with your family; pursue a completely new direction—perhaps one less stressful than the previous one.

RE-ENTERING/ENTERING THE MAINSTREAM WORKFORCE

Graduates

Irrespective of the discipline—a fairly broad Arts degree or one more specialised such as Law or Dentistry—a university education equips you with certain skills, and a certain way of assessing information and using it.

The ability to think both convergently and divergently, research and analytical skills, organisational skills, team-work, coordination—*any job you go for will tap into these areas*. No matter what your degree, if you can develop your report writing skills, communication skills, literacy and numeracy skills, and your ability to meet deadlines and to define and solve problems, you will find that you can transfer to other industries or sectors.

Any work experience is valuable. List your responsibilities and quantify them. Not: 'I worked at McDonalds as a customer service operator.' Give them something tangible: 'I worked at McDonalds, a job which involved cash handling, sometimes $4000 in a two-hour period.'

Think of your job search as an assignment. Identify targets, set targets, make some approaches that make sense to you. Where can I look? Who can I approach? How can I mount a campaign that will draw me to the attention of the sort of people I want? Map out a direction.

Start with your on-campus Careers Service which has a plethora of recruitment literature specifically aimed at people who are entering work for the first time from a university.

Size up every employment opportunity. What can I get out of this? And—remember it's a reciprocal relationship—what can I put into this? Perhaps you might have to make a start at a more modest level than you envisaged, or in a fringe industry. Try to get into an area where you can see an eventual connection so you can negotiate that experience into something more substantial or more in your chosen direction. You'll get the breaks you want as you build up your experience.

If you're a mature-age graduate, a package comprising your degree and the added plus of *previous industry experience* could actually give you the necessary edge.

Re-entering the workforce after a long absence

If you haven't worked in the mainstream for ten years, what have you done in that time that has provided you with valuable transferable skills?

Perhaps you've had to look after an aged relative and you can add home nursing to your skills. You might include: budgeting for a large family; gardening; cooking; and sewing. These are all skills which have the potential to transfer into the commercial sector. Also, don't forget the organisational skills you acquired managing a household. What about things you enjoy doing—could any relate to a potential job?

The key is to convince your potential employer that your skills and experience are relevant to the organisation. (This is where your preparation comes in. If you go without knowing anything about the company you are out of the race before you start.) You must be able to demonstrate that your past experience includes work similar to that on offer. Employers aren't mind-readers. If you say you were a secretary it might not convey the fact that you were responsible for six junior secretaries, your boss's travel arrangements, organising conferences, and liaison with the company's major suppliers.

You may need to undertake a refresher course or training to brush up on rusty skills or acquire new ones—to give you a competitive edge. *(See* Step 3, Capitalising On Your Assets.) There's no point in saying you *used* to be proficient on an IBM Selectric. Be familiar with the latest technology so you can say: 'I've just completed a meaty six-week course (on the latest software) and I'm up to advanced stage.'

Employers are interested in people who have good communication skills; who are interesting and interested. Raising children, involvement in community organisations, voluntary work, a tertiary education—all these demonstrate you are willing to take on responsibility and extend yourself beyond the immediate. Don't limit yourself to your old profession. Now is your chance to try a completely new tack.

A prominent television report focused on two new recruits in the police cadets. One was a social worker (female), the other a footballer (male). Each had skills that transferred to a position of public responsibility, accountability and teamwork. An arresting example of a lateral career move!

STOCKTAKING YOUR ASSETS

ASSESSING YOUR CURRENT POSITION

Okay, so you have established your particular motives for seeking a new career or getting your first one established.

The next step is to explore your own personal assets in terms of skills, attributes, experience, knowledge, and then your motivation.

It is generally accepted that people who are happiest and do well in their jobs are those who are passionate about their work. They really love what they do. Many people try to establish a career, or change their current position, without really looking closely at themselves to identify not only exactly what they have to offer, so they can articulate that to a new employer, but also to clarify *what it is they do best and what they most like doing.*

Why is that important? When evaluating a job, there are four potential outcomes.

THE FOUR SELECTION OUTCOMES

ACCEPTED ↑	TRUE POSITIVES	FALSE POSITIVES
	The Job 'Looks Right and is Right'	*(Type 1 Errors)* The Job 'Looks Right but is Wrong'
	(HIGH PERFORMANCE AND EASIER TO RECOGNISE)	(MARGINAL PERFORMANCE OR YOU LEAVE)
	TRUE NEGATIVES	**FALSE NEGATIVES**
	The Job 'Looks Wrong and is Wrong'	*(Type 2 Errors)* The job 'Looks Wrong but is Right'
REJECTED ↓	(CORRECTLY REJECTED BY YOU OR YOUR EMPLOYER)	(LOST TO COMPETITORS— HARDER TO RECOGNISE POTENTIALLY HIGH PERFORMANCE)

Outcome 1

The job looks right. And when you get closer to evaluating it, it is right. No real problem there. You've made a good match between what you think you want to do and what the job has to offer.

Outcome 2

The job looks wrong and it is wrong. Here the job doesn't look as though it is going to be what you want, and upon closer examination—either by talking to the prospective employer or getting the interview—it isn't what you want and you move on.

This is fairly straightforward so far. But now we arrive at two interesting outcomes where there are a great number of missed opportunities when people begin their job search.

Outcome 3

The job looks right, but it is wrong. Here, you are motivated by a title; the company's reputation; an industry you think is glamorous and exciting. However, once you get closer to that job, or worse still after you've accepted it, you find it's not the job for you. When you cut deeper into the daily, weekly and medium-term aspects of the role, the real match with expectations is not close enough. This has damaged many a career path.

Outcome 4

The final possible outcome is the biggest problem area of all. *The job looks wrong, but it is right.* Here, superficially, through a badly worded advertisement, a poorly conducted interview, or just because you have not been sufficiently open-minded about the job category, the industry, or the opportunity, you dismiss a role that could be a perfect match with your requirements.

So what is the solution? A major prerequisite is to take stock of your assets and find out who you really are.

Think of yourself as a motor car, and the job that fits most snugly (the one most appropriate to your goals, skills, knowledge, attributes, ambitions) as a tailor-made parking space. Take the time to have a really close look at yourself; take a look, as it were, under 'the bonnet of your mind' to find out what really makes you tick.

KNOWING YOURSELF

Knowing yourself is not just being aware that you are a compulsive clockwatcher and obsessive finger-tapper addicted to Tic Tacs (and promising yourself to do something about these annoying habits). It's recognising who you are and *what makes you tick*. When we don't stop to evaluate ourselves, particularly in a working environment, we can be our own worst enemy. Being so close to ourselves, we readily dismiss some experiences as not important when they are significant, and magnify others out of proportion.

Remember, a lot of the mismatches (the job looks right, but is wrong) have less to do with people being able to do the job, and more to do with their *not being compatible with the job,* and the goals, methodologies and culture of the organisation.

So before attempting to define the right job and right industry for you, it is necessary to cover some personal issues related to compatibility. When these issues are clear in your own mind, you will be able to identify jobs from Outcome 4 — the jobs that 'look wrong but are right'.

There are some key questions to ask yourself:

* *What do I want to do overall with my life? What do I want to achieve?* You need to quantify your personal goals and ambitions. Do you want to be rich? Famous? Both? Perhaps you want to be spiritually fulfilled? Or contribute to society in some way? Do you want to retire at forty and sail the world? Are you content to be behind the scenes or do you want to be in the front line of your chosen field?

- *What do I want to do in the next five years?* In corporate life we are often educated to believe that everyone must aspire to general management. There have been many cases of people pushing themselves to this end only to find that, when they got there, either they were not particularly good at it, or they didn't enjoy it.
- *What are my personal skills and attributes, and my natural talents, and can I utilise and blend them into my career decision?* If you have a natural head for figures, don't ignore it. Perhaps you've got a flair for writing, or an artistic bent. Maybe you sold door-to-door part-time during your studies, or there was a project you handled outside the normal routine of your job in which you excelled.
- *How good are my communication skills?* Do you prefer written or oral communication? Are you good at interpreting or conveying other people's directives? Do you enjoy communication on a one-to-one basis or one-to-group?
- *Am I a project-oriented person?* Are you someone who likes to complete a task and then go on to something new? Or are you more process-oriented, happy to be part of an ongoing chain of events and to complete your part of that chain intelligently?
- *What supervisory practices bring out the best* in *me?* Do you feel content taking instructions from others or are you happier giving orders to subordinates? Are you a leader or a follower?
- *What sort of people do I like to work for?* Would you prefer to work with dominant, authoritarian types or non-aggressive, diplomatic people? Do you enjoy working with people who are organised and hardworking, or those more relaxed in their attitude? How do you feel about people with extreme views on issues? Would that bother you?

- *What sort of culture do I operate best in?* Do you
  respond well to tight, clearly defined guidelines, or to a
  culture where you are given broad-based goals, and left
  alone to achieve them?

This last point in particular has been the downfall of both
employers and employees in many selection decisions. As
talented and capable as a person may be, being placed in an
environment where they expect (or need) to be managed
closely in the early stages, and instead are given a free rein,
can spell disaster. The opposite case leads to frustration, and
is equally a problem.

- *What sort of things motivate me?* Is it status?
  Recognition? Money? Often it is a combination of all
  three. Perhaps you are more motivated by intellectual
  stimulation; technical job content; or plenty of variety in
  your work.
- *What environment best suits me?* Are you happy working
  in a CBD high-rise building, or would you prefer the
  suburbs, or a country town? Are you best suited to
  regimented working hours or do you want the freedom
  to work whatever hours suit you? Perhaps you'd be
  happier doing contract work; or working on a part-time
  basis; or working from home?

The bottom line is that each of us is an 'unrepeatable
miracle'. It is your job to understand your particular miracle
better than anyone else, and more importantly to be able to
articulate it to potential employers to make it easy for them
to understand who you are, what you want, and what you
can contribute.

In marketing parlance this means you have to start selling
your *benefits*: what you *can do* for people—rather than your
features which rely on the employer to work out where you
can fit in. A *feature* might be that over-used generic, 'I'm

good with people'. A *benefit* will crystallise that further to the employer: 'I'm persuasive with people and therefore I believe I would be able to contribute positively to the team and to your customer services department'. *(See* Step 6 Section 1, Writing an Effective Résumé.)

ASSESSING YOUR STRENGTHS AND WEAKNESSES

We have covered the broader areas which relate to knowing yourself. Now we need to expand this further and define your strengths and weaknesses in the areas of your qualifications, experience, skills and knowledge. This is essential in foreseeing any gaps that might exist between you and your potential job.

A weakness is not your propensity for chocolate (at least in terms of a career) but rather something which either from lack of exposure, lack of interest, or just plain lack of ability, you are not good at. Your strengths are the things you are good at in terms of qualifications, experience, knowledge, skills and attributes.

Don't get despondent if there are a number of gaps. When hiring people, particularly those making a complete career change, many employers recognise there may be skills or knowledge gaps in relation to the position. As long as you have enough relevant strengths to support the area of weakness and the *potential* to fill those gaps fairly quickly, *don't disqualify yourself.* But you must be able to articulate, from your perspective, where the deficiencies are.

Potential employers are just as concerned about people not recognising the gaps between their experience and their skill base in relation to the particular job, as they are with the gaps themselves—so recognising they exist is half the battle. Draw up a simple checklist of your strengths and weaknesses and keep it in your job-search book. Then, as you evaluate each position, make a specific list pertinent to that position. For instance, your strengths could include an ability to:

- work in a team;
- work autonomously;
- work with a high level of accuracy—with an eye for detail;
- deal sensitively with people's feelings;
- operate a variety of software packages—spreadsheets, databases, word processing;
- design new systems;
- troubleshoot complex situations;
- sell;
- motivate teams or individuals;
- repair machinery;
- produce new ideas;
- entertain or perform in public;
- manage change;
- train other people;
- develop plans;
- evaluate options;
- negotiate or resolve conflict;
- manage/supervise people, things or information;
- budget.

FOR A MANAGEMENT POSITION YOUR STRENGTHS MIGHT INCLUDE AN ABILITY FOR:

- motivating teams;
- introducing change;

- controlling budgets;
- audit processes;
- market analysis;
- introduction of new practices—Quality Assurance (QA), Total Quality Management (TQM);
- maintaining regulatory controls;
- developing marketing plans;
- recruiting and training staff;
- making decisions.

This will also assist you further down the track in getting the interview and performing well in it. You recognise there are some weaknesses in relation to the position, but you have clearly considered them and are optimistic that you would be able to make up the appropriate ground with some training.

WHAT CAN I DO?

This is pretty straightforward and comes back to the hands-on skills, knowledge and attributes that you actually bring to a job. These are what the Human Resources Practitioner would call your *competencies*.

What qualifications do I have?

When you think about qualifications it must be in the broader sense of education and training. Don't just think of this as the part where you turn to the next page if you haven't got a university degree. Obviously if you wish to work as a computer programmer or analyse the stress factor in steel girders you will need specific qualifications. But in many areas qualifications are not relevant except to set you apart from another candidate who has no such formal qualification.

We recently chatted to the chief executive of a billion-dollar corporation. He qualified as an accountant but, in his opinion, the experience he gained whilst working for a fast food chain was one of the keys to his overall career success. At an early age it taught him the true meaning of customer service, marketing and operational controls.

So don't ignore those holiday jobs, part-time positions, the period when you were selling door-to-door, or the part-time courses. If you do have a university degree or post-graduate qualifications, go back through the curriculum and think about the course in more detail. There may be specific elements of that course which are relevant to some jobs and not others, and at the appropriate time you can draw on those to really enhance your chance for a particular role. Make sure you list every occasion that you accepted responsibility and when this was reflected in a more favourable result.

If you don't have the qualifications you need to pursue the career of your choice, then now is the time to resume your studies. Perhaps an MBA or DBA!! *But be warned: never claim you have qualifications you don't possess.* It's likely you'll be disqualified for misrepresentation even if you can do the job. If you really believe qualifications are not important in the position you're applying for, tell the truth— you might still get hired for other reasons!

What am I experienced to do?

Most people with ten to fifteen years' experience can adequately cover this in a three-to-four-page résumé. But at this stage of the game, when we are evaluating ourselves, it is important to go back chronologically through all your experience and highlight, in summary form, the skills and knowledge you have gained. You might have overlooked the fact that seven years ago, for six months, you managed a sales force or were part of a Research and Development team.

- Have your jobs been 'line' functions or 'staff' functions?
- Have you achieved results through people by persuasion in a 'staff' role, or did you manage them directly in a 'line' position?
- Did you inherit a job that was already established, or were you involved in a start-up phase?
- Were the people you managed new and relatively unskilled (highly motivated but low in competence); or were they fairly senior people who needed very little management and were given a high degree of autonomy (high competence, high motivation)?
- Perhaps you didn't manage anyone and you were more of a stand-alone expert?

Very few people bother to pull their experience apart in these dimensions. It will be invaluable in identifying those jobs that 'look wrong but are right'. And all of this detail will contribute to selling your benefits and not your features when you get to the interview stage.

Working knowledge

In the area of 'what can I do?' also comes knowledge. This means not only your technical knowledge, as in how the job works and what skills you have; also relevant here is industry knowledge and contacts, and an understanding of the way things get done. The ability to analyse another industry in terms of the skills, background, qualifications that make it tick, and the ability to compare yourself with that industry may enable you to identify a major opportunity for yourself and for your career.

Some of the best lateral job moves are made when evaluating this area and working out every conceivable alternative for feeding off the same industry or contact base you had in your past or present job. For example, you might work in manufacturing and you could join an organisation that services manufacturing companies. You may be in the public sector and associated with a particular segment of the community and then look at private companies that are servicing that same area. Or, as an even more lateral example, you might be a geologist with a knowledge of mining and minerals, and join the stockbroking firm that monitored your company's performance, as an analyst advising on the mining sector.

Skills

Skills are the things you can do well. They are also often things you enjoy, because if you get satisfaction from doing something you are most likely to do it well.

Skills are cumulative, they are built up gradually through repeated practice; they are sequential, each part is dependent on the previous part and influences the next. We acquire skills from everywhere in life: jobs, social interactions, sport, education—so you need to look at the broader picture and not just assess work-related skills. The ability to analyse, synthesise, work with facts and data, train people, grow plants and cook are all examples of skills we come up against in the commercial arena. Technical skills might be engineering and computing. Personal skills could include an ability to communicate effectively. Let's look at communication skills—these include oral, written and listening skills:

- Am I good or bad at communicating?
- In what way am I good at it? A better talker than listener, or vice versa?

- Am I good at *talking* to people or *listening* to them?
- Is that one-to-one, or one-to-group?
- Is it facilitating groups?
- Negotiating with groups?
- Presenting to groups?

All of these are different skills.

Personal skills quadrant

HIGHLY SKILLED	COMPETENT
NEEDS DEVELOPING	NO SKILLS

Look at the list of skills on the next page and sort them into the four quadrants by skill level. Once you have completed the first part of the exercise, highlight or underline the skills in each box which you are happiest using. There is often a strong relationship between skills we like to use and opportunities to use them. Don't turn your back on an opportunity which offers the chance to learn or develop a skill to which you may have had limited exposure.

When you are looking at a new position there are a few factors to be considered:

- If you are to be quickly effective in the new role, more than 70 per cent of the skills you will be required to use should be in the highly skilled or competent quadrant.
- If a role offers a 100 per cent skill fit with no opportunity to develop or master other skills or knowledge it may:
  – lack stimulation and challenge;
  – not contribute to your career development.

INFORMATION-GATHERING SKILLS INCLUDE:	PLANNING SKILLS INCLUDE:	DEVELOPMENT SKILLS INCLUDE:	PERFORMANCE/PRESENTATION SKILLS INCLUDE:
Analysing Classifying Researching Investigating Testing Evaluating Reviewing Critiquing Collecting Assessing Interpreting Editing Consulting	Organising Systematising Programming Arranging Prioritising Scheduling	Inventing Problem solving Conceptualising Directing Creating Visualising	Acting Performing Writing Publishing Painting Graphic design Drafting Decorating Playing an instrument Advertising Public speaking

NUMERICAL SKILLS INCLUDE:	PRODUCTION/MANUAL SKILLS INCLUDE:	MANAGEMENT SKILLS INCLUDE:	SELLING SKILLS INCLUDE:
Balancing Calculating Counting Recording Auditing	Operating Building Assembling Installing Inspecting	Supervising Training Developing ideas Manipulating Delegating Demonstrating Planning Formulating strategy Co-ordinating Motivating Initiating Organising Directing Reviewing Hiring/Firing Negotiating Counselling Helping Guiding	Convincing Demonstrating Persuading Closing Assessing Relationship building

HOW TO MAKE THE MOST OF WHAT YOU'VE GOT

Career management is a very personal process. Various tools can aid it immensely—especially to give you personal insight—but only you can set goals, plan, activate and review your progress. Life goals and career goals are inextricable. *Nothing can be achieved without your commitment to yourself and your career.*

At twenty-five, single and with few commitments, your needs will be different to those at forty-five or as you approach retirement; and the concerns of someone who is actually employed, even in a dull job, may differ to those of someone who has been unemployed for a considerable time. However, the fundamental skills required for career management do not change.

It requires individual initiative and a proactive approach. A willingness to explore, plan ahead and take action—even when this means taking risks—can make a difference in the quality of your career and your life. *High achievers think actively, not passively*—they are always searching for a better way, a better life, a higher goal.

KEY WORDS TO KEEP IN MIND DURING THE JOB SEARCH:

Research Whether buying a computer or planning a career move, research is the all-important key. *To fail to plan is to plan to fail!*

Flexibility You may have to rethink work in terms of full-time, part-time, temporary, contracting, consulting, partnering, self-employment and retraining. Being open to different types of working arrangements is likely to enhance your employment prospects.

Diversification You may have to be willing to move from your traditional area of work in order to achieve a long-term goal. For example, you may have a retail banking background and be keen to stay in the financial services industry. To do that may mean temporarily forgoing a high-status title for an opportunity to prove your worth in a different part of the industry.

Lateral thinking about industry and the public sector Consider transferring your existing skills into another arena: a former commander in the defence forces with skills in leadership, administration, strategic planning and operations can become an efficient manager of other resources; for example in a logistics role in the private sector.

Adaptability about your skills Identify skills where you can adapt your expertise to another area. If your forte is synthesising information and you have good keyboard skills, but lack the ability to present that information coherently, investigate learning these skills to plug the gap. The new knowledge worker of the twenty-first century is never going to stop training (learning).

Mobility Job security is the capacity to learn fast, to be mobile.

There's no such thing as a secure job any more, only secure people.

The smart employees of this decade will be constantly evaluating what they can learn from their present job and company to help them make the next five-year move. Only 'smarter' employers who are constantly changing and learning as an organisation will be able to keep those knowledge workers (so called because their knowledge is transportable) within the organisation at each stage of their development.

MAKE GETTING A JOB YOUR MAIN JOB

If you're really serious about getting a job or making an effective career move you should treat your search like a full-time job. This means that if you're between jobs you should devote thirty-five hours a week just to get activity and interviews going. If you're working full-time then use your spare time constructively to conduct your job search—don't expect it to happen by accident.

Don't just think about it: ask around, network, make confidential appointments, *be proactive*. Don't assume others are working on your behalf. And don't just use one method of approach and expect an organisation to snap you up. You need to explore opportunities and you need to make every possible approach concurrently.

Get up, get your act together and prepare yourself as if you are going to 'work'.

Setting up a separate area to work in

If you are job-hunting from home there is nothing more time wasting than getting bogged down in the day-to-day machinations of the household. If you haven't got a spare room, choose a corner and make it your own. This is where you'll keep your workbook and all your research material. Set yourself specific hours. Have an agreement with your housemates or family that this is the time you are doing your job search. Keep a telephone within easy reach.

If it's impossible to work from home, perhaps you can arrange access to a friend's house twice a week. But do something tangible to give yourself the right environment to do this job professionally.

Organising yourself

One of the reasons outplacement or career transition management programs have been so successful is the organisation they bring to the job search. If you take identical twins with the same skill sets, the one on the outplacement program will get a job faster. Why?

A recent survey showed that job-seekers on an outplacement program spent an average of thirty-one hours per week actively looking for a job whilst those who were not involved in a program spent less than ten hours.

If you don't have the benefit of such a program, you *can* duplicate it. Once you have made the decision to move and you have worked out who you are and what you want, then it becomes a numbers game—a case of increasing the probabilities with more irons in the fire. Being organised is therefore essential.

In the Appendices we have outlined some basic forms to help you to compile your workbook, but here are the golden rules:

- *Record everything:* Keep notes/files on every letter sent, every telephone call made, every approach, every rejection, every interview granted. Write reports for yourself on the attitudes you perceived when phoning for feedback on your interview—the points that seem to have impressed and those that went down like a lead balloon. Be in control of your job search, and don't leave anything to chance.

  If you start to send out half-a-dozen letters a day and make twenty calls a week, when momentum starts to build in your job search and people start to call you back (I assume you are expecting to be successful?), you are going to look pretty silly if you can't quickly refer to the relevant letter or telephone call and sound composed, intelligent and ready for action.

- Each time you send out your résumé, *consider it a separate campaign*—plan the attack and follow through. Only *your* effort can ensure you'll get the right job.

- *Be disciplined* about putting in a minimum of five hours a day on your job search. Treat it as a job in its own right and get serious about building a wave. Don't be frustrated in the first two or three weeks because it will build slowly. Not everyone will drop everything to get back to you when your résumé or telephone message comes into their busy working life. But sooner or later, if you are positioning yourself appropriately, the tide will turn.

Job-seekers who put one or two, sometimes five, irons in the fire a week, often get despondent after two or three weeks because nothing is happening. *A job search builds in momentum, typically generating interviews in the second and third months.*

- *Set goals:* without a goal it's very hard to get motivated. You find yourself directionless, floundering, wasting valuable time. Of course your ultimate goal is a successful job search, but to get there you need to set yourself smaller, more easily accomplished goals.

Make it a **SMART** goal:

S	the goal has to be Specific
M	Manageable
A	Achievable
R	Realistic
T	Time bound

Write down your goals and tick them off. A goal can be as simple as a list of what to do tomorrow.

- *Document your day,* which could include:
  - telephone calls;
  - letters;
  - cutting out job advertisements;
  - recording names and contacts from your diaries over the last few years to develop a personal network list (*see* Step 4 Section 6, The networking approach);
  - research on specific companies.
- *Document your weekly game plan,* which could include:
  - responding to ten advertised jobs by sending your résumé and individually fashioned letters of introduction;
  - arranging and completing a minimum of two interviews;

- sending your résumé to at least five companies which have impressed you after reading newspaper and magazine articles about them;
- discussing job leads with two personal contacts in your industry or profession and follow through with a résumé if appropriate;
- talking with industry personnel in general about movements and possible job openings. Send your résumé to the personnel department with a covering letter showing your enthusiasm for joining their organisation. Ask for an information interview.

There is no one task which should be tackled first. You have to know the various alternatives, including the hidden opportunities, and *tackle them concurrently*. This is the way to get the greatest coverage in the shortest time.

Writing to companies after reading an article about them is *one of the hidden opportunities*. Consider features in business magazines and the business section of newspapers as job advertisements. Expansions, new products, mergers, personnel changes, office moves: all these could provide employment opportunities.

If you read about a person who has just been promoted, wait a few weeks and write to that specific person expressing your interest in the organisation.

Getting this job is the most important job you'll ever have. Unless your job is a specific one which only comes up once a year, then it's a case of input versus output. No effort equals no response. And be prepared for (but never anticipate) rejection.

By the way, that old chestnut, 'Should I take some time off to sit on a beach and think about my career, or get straight into the job search?' is a simple one to answer. Unless there is a strong reason for you to have a rest and straighten your mind out, get into it right away and take your holiday once you have a job offer. You can usually negotiate a short delay before starting a new position and, if not, think of it this way—obtaining *the right job* is as good as a holiday.

Define your objectives

Draw up the following lists:

Job satisfaction
List those job conditions and situations which are most likely to provide you with job satisfaction.

Career directions
After careful consideration of all the information that you have available, list in order of priority your possible career direction.

Jobs/careers—now
List, in order of priority, your ideal jobs/careers.

Jobs/careers in five years time
List, in order of priority, your ideal jobs/careers in five years time.

Personal development
Identify the personal and/or formal development you will need to achieve your longer term goals.

Organisations

Having identified the kind of career you want, what drives you and what you require to be satisfied in a career, now think carefully about the kind of organisation that best suits you—in terms of its ability to provide you with the career that you want, and in terms of its ability to match your own personal style. List the criteria the organisation should have. Consider such factors as size, culture, rewards, future prospects, economic sectors, management style, ongoing career opportunities.

Bearing in mind your criteria for the ideal organisation, name those organisations that provide careers you want to pursue, and for whom you would like to work.

TAKING CARE OF YOURSELF

There's an old adage: ideally, don't change your home, your relationship and your job all at the same time. Unless you have some stability as an anchor in at least one of these areas, it will be difficult to make a change successfully.

If you are not coping with the personal side of your life, and it's detrimental to your finding a job, then you should really talk to someone you can trust or seek professional counselling. At the very least read something from the abundance of literature available on the subject. It takes work to get your life in order, but here are some suggestions to help you cope with the stress:

- Watch your diet in terms of your intake of caffeine, alcohol, tobacco, sugar—anything which has a negative physiological effect.
- Establish a routine of physical exercise, ie. two to three times a week, assuming of course you are basically in good health.
- Practise a regular form of relaxation.
- Identify other means of releasing stress—listening to music, reading, meditation, eating out or dancing.
- If you're going a short distance, walk! It's good exercise and a terrific way to clear the cobwebs.

- Seek input from outside people. Don't carry the burden alone; bounce your problems/fears off family and friends.
- If you feel you need professional help, go out and get it. Talk to your doctor.
- Maintain high personal standards. You never know when opportunity is going to knock—when you might open the door to that ideal job.
- 'All work and no play . . .' Make sure you reward yourself when you've put in a good day's job search.

Outside help in the job search

Getting free professional advice

If you don't seem to be achieving much by yourself, utilise those whose job it is to help you, free of charge: your librarian for research assistance; a community careers adviser; Centrelink Employment Service. The State government also runs vocational guidance counselling services.

There are also various community-based organisations which provide practical assistance for job-seekers through seminars and training programs. These are usually free of charge.

Professional help for a fee

Professional résumé writers usually charge $150–$350 per page. Check the telephone book or the employment section of the newspaper.

Some recruitment firms offer career counselling on an informal basis, but if you want specific interview training and career guidance counselling you will probably find the service available to you for a nominal hourly rate through the human resources division of recruitment companies which have Career Transition Management (CTM) and outplacement services. These companies sometimes run candidate-paid CTM programs which generally last for two to three days and cost around $400–$1000. Alternatively, you could contact the local branch of the Australian Association of Career Counsellors.

HOW TO DEVELOP AND MAINTAIN CONFIDENCE

Lack of confidence is one of the most pervasive forces holding back careers. Everywhere there are people who miss out because they doubt their own capabilities. This comes from a feeling of inadequacy, a fear of being unable to meet responsibilities and take on something bigger. Remember, learning is growing and to learn you have to take on tasks that are new. We may fail from time to time, but we learn and grow from our failures.

Let's face it—most people, if given the opportunity, would like to have more confidence in themselves, but it's not always easy to generate. After all, it's not just something a person can create for themselves. *Or is it?*

The truth is that confidence—having a positive self-attitude, feeling self-reliant and assured, being able to tackle a problem with enthusiasm and vitality—is something over which you *do* have control.

So how do you build up your confidence? There is a great deal of evidence to suggest that successful people, in all walks of life, have the ability to create more positive 'self-talk' than others.

Here are a few ways to improve your 'internal' self-talk:

- Create a picture in your mind of yourself as a success by remembering the things you *have* done well, however small. Hold on to this image tenaciously and don't let it fade. No matter how badly things seem to go, keep drawing on your 'success' image.

- Whenever you have any negative thoughts that overshadow you, cancel them with positive thoughts. They could be memories of being congratulated by your boss on doing a good job; an interview that went well. They could be feelings of personal achievement or mental pictures of a favourite scene that make you feel at peace with yourself.

- Often in times of stress we imagine obstacles that will prevent us making a success of our lives. Stop and use your internal powers of persuasion to dispel them.

- You might admire and want to emulate a successful person, but don't allow yourself to be awestruck to the point where you really believe you can't match that success. Remember, nobody can do it as well as you. Most people, despite their self-confident demeanour, are doubtful about themselves at some time. Select and mix with successful and positive people. Stay away from the losers—they are always critical and project negativity.

- If you have deep inferiority blocks, don't be afraid to gain the assistance of a competent counsellor. Self-knowledge often leads to cure.

- Make a true assessment of your ability, then raise it 10 per cent. It's not being egotistical, it's just a case of thinking positively. You'll never improve your situation unless you create a realistic goal and aim to achieve it.

Don't let a situation defeat you even before you confront the reality of it. Draw on the power of positive thinking. The way you approach life is up to you.

If you choose to be confident and happy, you'll be comfortable and in control. Tackle life in a positive manner and you can overcome most obstacles.

Be enthusiastic and single-minded about your convictions and where you channel your energy, and you'll get results. Okay, you say, it's easy for you—I've lost my job! But you'll never get another one if you're negative and defeatist. Look ahead, not back.

Whatever you can do, or dream you can ... begin it.
Boldness has genius, power and magic in it.

GOETHE

WE CAN ALL CHANGE— IF WE WANT TO!

What can you do about those personal traits that have been your downfall in previous jobs? Can you do anything to change them? Yes, you can. Here are a few methods for improving some of your actions/abilities:

* *Improving your memory and concentration*—Read a passage from a book and test yourself by writing down the details of what you've just read. Did you get them all? Write down the ones you missed. Now, read the passage again. Did you remember more details this time?

  When you come across a difficult word, write it down. At the end of the piece, look up each word in the dictionary and write down the meaning. Every night, cover the explanation and try to remember the correct meaning. This way you can improve your concentration, your comprehension and add to your word skills.

- *Too emotional at work*—You must learn to separate your private from your business life. Employers are not interested in employees who spend their work hours organising their social life and dealing with relationship problems. If you're going through a difficult patch, find a colleague who is prepared to talk you through the situation in a lunchbreak. If your work is suffering, and you have a good relationship with your boss, discuss your dilemma but don't expect things to be made easy for you on the job. Try breaking your work day into specific tasks for specific short periods—it's a good way to keep your mind from straying.

- *You're shy*—Then you must work on boosting your confidence. Monitor your negative thinking. Do you spend time worrying about your inability to achieve? Do you let others speak for you when you have your own opinions? Do you always think whatever you have done isn't good enough? Work out *when* you think such things, *what* situation you're in, and *why* you do so. Once you can recognise when your lack of confidence most often surfaces, you'll be more able to address the problem.

- *You're tactless*—Courtesy and tact are communication skills that are 'other person' oriented. If you're a very 'me' person, you're likely to find tact doesn't come easily. You need self-control. Stop and think *before* you speak. Could what you're about to say be offensive to anyone around you? Is there a way of tempering your conversation so your comments don't appear to be so egocentric or insensitive? Place yourself in the other person's position— how would I feel if this was said to me?

  If you're at your worst in a confrontational situation, put off discussing the problem until you've cooled down.

COPING WITH REJECTION

Job-hunting, particularly when you're out of work and *need* the job, can be most depressing. You start with all the confidence in the world, but as you receive each rejection—and you will be rejected, no matter how good you are (or worse, you won't hear back at all)—you're likely to feel doubts about your personal ability. Then you'll find any excuse to put off that first phone call. You may have to look up *topiary* in the dictionary, but suddenly shaping your hedge or pot plant into a dinosaur becomes an obsession. And by the time you've searched out the ideal clippers for the job it's mid-afternoon and you can rationalise taking the rest of the day off. Before long, it's not just a day, it's a week, then a month. And so on.

You can't afford to allow yourself to fall into this quagmire of rejection. You can't afford to allow your self-esteem to drop because just when you've given up, a real opportunity will arise. If you don't stay positive and 'up', you won't be able to seize it.

The job market is highly competitive, there are usually many applicants for any job, and new employers are selective. Often the decision isn't against you, but for someone else who was simply a better 'fit'. *That's why it's so important to get feedback: to understand why you might have been rejected, learn from your experience, and improve your approach*—assuming that's the reason you didn't get the job offer.

If you receive too many rejections you might have to accept you are going about it the wrong way:

- Maybe the job market has changed. Get some input from people who work in your field. What skills are they currently looking for? What background?
- How are you labelling yourself? Do a bit of research. Let's take a simple example: a typist. If you talked to five employers they would probably say: 'We haven't employed a typist for years; what we have now are word process operators'. A similar skill has just been repackaged so you need to make sure your skills are recognised in a way that benefits you.
- If you've been unemployed for a while, check your approach. Perhaps it's time to change your tack, apply for different sorts of jobs in a different way.
- Be careful about getting into a set pattern. If something is not working, don't keep on doing it.
- If you've been getting negative responses to your résumé, and then suddenly two people want to talk to you, find out what you did differently and repeat it.
- Having numerous and new irons in the fire can keep you quietly optimistic. Always make sure something new is happening to keep you focused on tomorrow rather than yesterday.

6 SURVIVING FINANCIALLY

If you are no longer receiving a regular income you really need to take immediate stock of your finances and, more importantly, your expenditure. Some of you will have received large payouts. Most of the major finance companies advertise regularly, offering financial services, including free seminars. Don't dismiss retirement seminars: they're not necessarily only for retirees. Make sure you research the market thoroughly. You probably want independent financial advice rather than a company linked to specific products, such as a bank.

If you are relying on government assistance, you should register with the relevant department the minute you are made redundant, as there is often a waiting period. Your local Centrelink office will be able to supply information on what you must do to claim benefits and can also assist you in looking for a job.

Basic budgeter

In the Appendices you will find an example of a Basic Budgeter (pages 246–247). Fill it out using last year's expenses as a guideline. To cover inflation and contingencies add 10 per cent to your total expenses. Now subtract your expenses from your income to give you a profit/loss figure for the year. (Use last year's tax return to help you work out your total income.)

If your total annual spending (including your savings and investments) equals 100 per cent or less of your income, your finances are probably in relatively good condition. Depending on your financial goals, you may want to reaassess expenditures to increase your savings each year.

If your expenditure is more than 100 per cent, you have a problem. You're either carrying excessive amounts of debt or dipping into your savings to cover some of your expenses.

Although cutting back on your savings may seem the easiest way to adjust your budget, try not to do it. If your analysis indicates you're spending too much, you have other options:

- Consider refinancing your mortgage, consolidating your loans or streamlining your insurance coverage.

- Keep track of your cash expenditures so you don't underestimate this portion of your cash flow.
- Don't panic and cut back all your expenses at once. Establish limits within which you and your family can live, and plan to reassess your cash flow on a regular basis.
- Consult your financial adviser, who may have other money-savings ideas.

There's no mystery. To achieve financial security you must save a portion of your income on a regular basis.

Selecting a suitable financial planner

Free advice isn't always the way to go—if you are seeking a professional service, be prepared to pay for it. In your search for a reliable and experienced financial adviser, you may find the following questions helpful in guiding your choice:

- What licences do you and your firm hold to provide financial advice?
- Who owns the firm and what is your role?
- How long have you been involved in financial planning? What are your qualifications and experience?
- How are your fees structured? Do you charge for:
  - initial consultation;
  - a portfolio;
  - annual or regular interviews;
  - amending a portfolio.
- Will you or your firm receive a fee or any other incentive payment from the investments I make?
- How do you select the investments you recommend and how do you determine what is suitable for me?
- Do you provide a written report? If so, what information does it contain? Can you show me an example of a typical report?

- What other services am I entitled to if I become a client of your firm?
- Can you provide me with the names of some existing clients who would be prepared to endorse your company and its services?

Be wary of reluctance to answer any of these questions and watch for these dangers:

- an unlicensed and inexperienced practitioner;
- hidden and/or expensive fees;
- recommendation of only high-commission products;
- a lack of research facilities and a lack of an independent approach in selection of investment products.

TRAINING AND RETRAINING 7

Because we are in a rapidly changing work environment it is important to look ahead.

Remember the typing pool? It doesn't exist any more. In fact, keyboard skills, once the domain of the secretary, are now attached to management. To be in control of one of the biggest sources of information, it is now desirable for people in management to be computer literate, and that means using a keyboard too!

In the present day workplace you can't afford to become complacent. Look for every opportunity to add to your skills. Take advantage of on-the-job training and adult education courses that will give you new skills.

Build on your existing skills. For example, if you are a good communicator talking to people on a one-to-one basis but you would like to talk to groups, find a good way to gain that experience. Join a Toastmasters group or a public-speaking course. Or simply volunteer more often, in your present job, to make group presentations.

Computer courses are available through technical colleges and private providers. Again, research is the key word. Make sure the program is suitable for your needs. Make sure you have access to a computer on which to practise your newly acquired skills—there is no point in splurging out on a computer course if you can't immediately utilise what you've learnt because you'll forget it. If you decide to buy a computer, make sure it can cope with your needs; don't just take the seller's word for it—research and network!

Universities, TAFE (Technical and Further Education) colleges and adult education services offer a range of courses, both degree and non-degree. Ring them direct or check your local library for their handbooks which detail the subjects, qualifications and enrolment procedures. The Federal Government provides assistance for full-time secondary and tertiary studies. The major program of assistance is known as Youth Allowance. Check your eligibility through your local Centrelink office.

Most TAFE courses are available on a full-time or part-time basis and many can be studied by correspondence. TAFE colleges are located throughout Australia.

The Federal Government has specific programs, run through Centrelink, to assist the long-term unemployed and other disadvantaged people. You may be eligible for financial assistance for study, job training and travel expenses.

Voluntary work is one way to stop your skills atrophying and may also help acquire a few new ones. It has the added advantages of:

- demonstrating you are a fairly motivated person;
- broadening your network of contacts;

- extending your range of skills;
- gaining valuable experience in a new area;
- filling a gap in your résumé;
- building your self-confidence;
- being in the right place at the right time for paid employment;
- increasing your confidence while refreshing your existing skills;
- easing you back into the workforce after a lengthy break.

Apart from approaching a non-profit organisation direct, there are various organisations in each State, such as the Volunteer Centre, which place people in voluntary work, matching the range of skills the individual has to offer with the organisations which take on volunteers. Some centres will also provide background training.

Volunteers can undertake work in a wide range of jobs, such as publicity and promotions, hospital respite care, welfare counselling, word processing, data entry, community arts such as graphic design and photography, teaching English as a second language, and general management of organisations through administration and committee work.

You could choose to work unpaid in the private sector but this is difficult for most employers: they may be accused of exploitation, as there are *award rates*.

Part-time, temporary or casual work is another way of using your skills while looking for full-time employment. (*See* Step 9, Being Your Own Boss.)

STEPS TO SUCCESSFULLY SELLING YOURSELF

Most selling technique experts will tell you there are five steps towards a successful sale: approach, interest, need, desire and close.

- To sell anything, salespeople have to know who they're approaching—even though they may never have met them before. You must use the same tactic when selling yourself for a job. So how do you find your potential employer? The same way salespeople find potential buyers: through *research*. Using the information in Step 4, Where to Invest Your Assets, you'll know exactly how to research the job market and pinpoint potential employers.

- Remember, *you* are the product. You must create *interest* in yourself, for the potential buyer. You'll do this by writing an appealing résumé and letter of introduction. Step 6, Packaging Your Assets, will show you how.

- If there is a *need* for the product then you are halfway there. But you still have to persuade the buyer you are worth interviewing.

- Creating a *desire* in your potential employers—if they are not in the market for a new employee—is tough, but with the right approach you could still make a sale.

- Finally, you must *close* the sale by being offered the job. Where most salespeople fail is in their inability to close the interview by asking for the order: in this case, the job. Doing this is particularly difficult, but crucial to your success. Step 7, Selling Your Assets, will outline the necessary skills.

So what makes you a better candidate than everyone else who's searching for your job? The fact that you are:

- more focused!
- better prepared!
- have more irons in the fire!
- offering more options!

In short, the odds are already swinging in your favour.

The next chapters will detail how to research the market thoroughly and target your specific job. Don't waste your energy by not being prepared.

RESEARCHING THE JOB MARKET

Before we talk about which industries are on the move and which are becoming dinosaurs, we have to reflect on the changing nature of the workforce, the global economy, and the impact it has on jobs and people.

Many modern organisations are 'outsourcing' functions. This has led to a spate of new growth companies—small or medium-sized—that are taking over work previously done by the larger conglomerate or government organisation internally.

Printing and photocopying rooms are now being managed by external printing companies. Consulting or accounting firms are taking over the accounting that was once performed in-house. Government-run transport organisations outsource the repair and maintenance of buses and trains to private companies specialising in that field.

So new career opportunities can spring out of established, conventional industries in a different guise while other organisations are reducing their numbers! Don't take anything for granted: the pace of change is too rapid for that.

The emergence of the two-income family and more flexible working arrangements have also opened up new areas. Regular jobs that were traditionally done within the home or by (unpaid) housewives have developed into businesses that provide jobs for other people. For instance, five years ago how many people had laundry or dry-cleaning delivered and picked up from home? There are now companies with names like Wife Without Strings or Dial-A-Wife, created by people who recognised the changing nature of work and the opportunities available because of those changes. Lawn cutting, gardening, and house maintenance services have expanded to provide complete home-care packages. The growth of these mini-industries has also created jobs in the sales, marketing and operational areas.

Finally, before we move on to naming specific industries or job functions that appear to have a promising future, we should bear in mind that with organisational structures that are flatter and leaner, and with high technology providing information at the fingertips, there is a need for more flexible people with broadly based skills in the workforce.

In the past, warehousing and distribution often covered two or three distinct functions: inventory control, control of the warehouse in terms of goods received and despatched, and the financial management of those transactions. These were usually handled by a specialist in the accounts department. These days, those jobs can be done by one executive with a database which automatically calculates stock to be re-ordered and when it should be despatched. Upon despatch the same data network produces the documents required to charge the customer and make payment to the supplier.

So when you look for new career opportunities, don't just chase them in the new 'sexy' industries: *your* career might lie in a restructured but traditional area.

ONLINE JOB SEARCH

The online world is rapidly becoming the easiest way to search and apply for jobs twenty-four hours a day, seven days a week, without geographic or time barriers.

As the Internet and online population is now greater than the population of many countries, employers and employees alike are flocking to online recruitment and networking. We hope that the following information will provide you with a springboard for diving right into online recruitment opportunities.

Privacy and security online

Before entering the world of online recruitment, privacy and security are two fundamental aspects that every online job-seeker should be aware of.

The following checklist should be adhered to when you are in the process of online job searching.

- If you post your résumé to a public (that means access available to all) recruitment web site, be aware that not all people viewing these details may be who you expect. You should only post personal details such as name, address and phone number to web sites that have in-built security and are password protected.

- If you post your résumé to a web site (a secure one, of course), ensure you have the ability to remove it as soon as you have completed your job search. This will prevent unnecessary correspondence and phone calls.

- Make sure you have the ability to stipulate who sees your résumé, eg. either send it to a professional, registered recruitment firm, or post it to a web site where you are allowed to select who sees your details from a list of employers. In other words, you DO NOT want your current employer having access to your résumé in a list of available candidates.

- Always use a secure (non-employer monitored) email account to communicate online with prospective recruiters. Options include:
  - www.hotmail.com
  - www.yahoo.mail.com

- Identity thieves are alive and surfing on the Internet. Basically, identity thieves want your life history to use for credit and reference checks. To prevent this always use secure web sites, and always remove your résumé after you have found a job.

Building a résumé

The reason recruiters and many employers want to receive your résumé electronically is because they will store your details electronically in a candidate database. This allows them to search and match your skills against the positions they have vacant instantly.

There are a few basic rules to remember when building an electronic résumé:

- Always create as plain text or ASCII, eg. if the employer only has Word Version 3 and you create a Word Version 6 file, the employer will not be able to open the file.

- Do not underline headings.
- Do not use italics unnecessarily.
- Do not use tables unneccessarily.
- Always format in portrait style.
- Do not include graphics or photographs of yourself.

If all of the above appears too complicated there are some web sites on the Internet that offer résumé-building facilities. These services should always be free of charge. They are designed to assist you to build a professional online résumé that is user-friendly, highlights key words and is in a format that is accepted by almost all employers. The one exception to this rule is government organisations, where you are usually expected to fill out a standard government online application.

Listed below are national and international recommended job sites that you can register your details with:

- www.JobNet.com.au
- www.Monster.com.au
- www.morganbanks.com.au
- www.ajb.dni.us
- www.careermosaic.com
- www.Monster.com
- www.TAPS.co.uk
- www.Jobsite.co.uk

Reasons to use the Internet in your job search

- *Free access to information and resources.* With access costs to the Internet becoming more and more competitive, more people are beginning to take advantage of the thousands of free resources and job listings, as well as résumé-writing tips, interview tips and other career guidance tools.
- *Using key words to find jobs.* Newspapers provide job listings; however, they can require extensive visual

scanning. The Internet, on the other hand, allows you to search job databases using key words for fast, effective retrieval of jobs.

- *Access to company vacancies.* The majority of large companies now provide a set page on their web site dedicated to vacancies within their organisation, or provide a direct link to their HR department. Many of these vacancies are company-wide and are not geographically restricted.
- *Networking.* The most important part of getting a job is making contacts and where best to do so than on the world's largest electronic network!
- *Tomorrow's information today.* While newspapers publish a job section on a weekly basis, and the information published is only valid as to the day of print, the Internet provides you with daily updates of vacancies worldwide.
- *No boundaries!* The Internet has no geographic or time barriers, and access is available twenty-four hours a day, 365 days a year.
- *Leading-edge skills.* Organisations, especially businesses, are rushing to get onto the Internet. They see opportunities for advertising, possible commercial markets and a vast wealth of information that they can tap in to. Using the Internet in your job search demonstrates to the employer your familiarity and skill with this new market area.
- *Searching for jobs using global technology.* There is more to searching for a job on the Internet than giving it to a large online job bank/employment page. You need to have a plan of attack. There are some specific job-related web pages on the Internet that you can use to source the job you are looking for. These are as follows:
  - recruitment websites;
  - employment jobs bank;
  - online classified;

- company home pages;
- electronic journals;
- news groups;
- mailing lists;
- search engines.

Recruitment websites

A home page for a recruitment firm will display general or industry-specific jobs for you to view. A recruitment web site of merit will provide you with the ability to apply for positions online.

Employment jobs bank

An employment jobs bank represents a site on the Internet where both recruitment firms and employers can post job vacancies. A usual service provided by some jobs banks allows you to post your résumé in a secure area, so only employers and recruitment firms of your choice can view your details.

Online classified

An online classified web site is what we refer to as a newspaper online. Many of the major newspapers now sport their own web site displaying employment adverts that they have printed in the press. If you apply to a classified web site your résumé will normally be directed to the recruitment firm or employer who has placed that particular vacancy.

Electronic journals

Electronic journals are industry-based publications normally managed by a society or organisation. These are usually free and provide industry-related articles and possible networking contacts together with job listings.

News Groups

Internet news groups are public bulletin boards where you are free to post requests for employment or vacancies. The jobs news groups have jobs, résumés, discussions on how to find a job, and general career information. Industry-specific news groups provide an excellent opportunity for networking. (For a comprehensive list of news groups go to http:\\www.listz.com)

Mailing lists

Similar to news groups, mailing lists cover a broad variety of topics and industries. Occasionally job postings can be found. However, their main benefit is to establish networking contacts, keep abreast of industry trends and receive updates on who's who in a specific industry.

Search engines

There are three main ways to use a search engine:

- enter key words;
- use subject categories;
- assess recruitment sites through banner advertising.

The following are some of the more popular search engines in Australia:

- www.yahoo.com.au
- www.altavista.digital.com.au
- www.anzwers.com.au

The don'ts of online job search

- DON'T send a general résumé without a cover letter stating where and when you are available for work and, most importantly, what type of job you are seeking.

- DON'T send your résumé on an email to multiple organisations. Remember, the top of every email you send will show who else you have sent your details to. Mass emails do not create a good impression.
- DON'T ask general questions like 'how do I get a job' or 'do you have job vacancies'. Be more specific and remember you may be one of thousands of emails that an organisation receives weekly. The more specific your question the more specific the answer.
- DON'T email your résumé to a prospective employer or recruitment firm in the latest WP version. Often the most basic is best, for example a basic text file (.txt) is likely to be accessible by all versions of computer users. While sending your résumé in the latest version of Word 2000 may make you think you are technologically up to date, it will simply frustrate the potential employer if they are unable to access your document.

The do's of electronic applications

- DO use key words that show you match the position requirements.
- DO keep the résumé short and sharp. Remember, it is an initial contact only.
- DO put your most important skills at the beginning of the résumé.
- DO keep the format of the résumé simple.
- DO use only plain fonts, no italics or underline and no borders.
- DO remember to provide your email address and telephone number. The aim is to be contactable, so make sure your email address is correct on your résumé.
- DO always keep a hard copy of your résumé close at hand for incoming enquiries.

Where to access the Internet

The following is a list of locations where you can easily access the Internet:

- local library (usually free);
- State library (usually free);
- universities (usually free);
- government employment centres (usually free);
- local councils (sometimes free);
- Internet cafés (not free).

Where to get free email access

If you use the Internet and email at work, be aware that many organisations track all outgoing and incoming emails. Therefore if you need to keep your job search private you shouldn't use your work-based email account. A more private alternative is a free web-based email account. Some web sites where you can create a global free email account that can be accessed from any computer in the world with Internet access are as follows:

- http:\\www.hotmail.com
- http:\www.email.com
- http:\www.myemail.com
- http:\www.yahoo.com

RECOGNISING WHERE AN INDUSTRY IS POSITIONED

There are usually three uneven stages an industry will experience before it has run its course: birth, growth and maturity. Depending on the industry, this life cycle could take decades to grow (as with the computer industry), or mature overnight (the compact disc industry).

There are advantages and disadvantages in joining a company at *any* of these stages—it depends on your career plan. It's not just the job that's important, because jobs cross the spectrum of most industries. What is important is your potential within those industries.

- Does the industry offer advancement?
- Will it improve your quality of life?
- What about mobility and being noticed in the organisation?
- Does it offer good working conditions?

You need to analyse which of these stages is right for you.

New industries offer high risk but also high reward environments. They are usually launched to meet perceived market demands which haven't been proven. If they work, employees do well. If their promise doesn't come to fruition, employees could find themselves without jobs. However, if the excitement and the thrill of being a mover in a new industry suits your personality, and you perceive you can improve your management/technical ability at a great pace, then new industries could be ideal. You'll probably have to show some entrepreneurial zest and be prepared to work long hours to earn your rewards.

Growth industries usually offer the most balanced opportunities because they provide relative security and stability along with high rewards, challenges and the potential to be noticed. How do you recognise a growth industry? One market observer suggests you look for an annual growth of about 8 per cent. Other things to look for are new markets, new facilities, and expansions to sales and products. Because growth industries offer a win–win situation, they are targeted most by motivated job-seekers and the competition is strong. You'll need excellent job-search skills, superior qualifications, and the ability to prove you have the entrepreneurial spirit to crack one of these industries.

Mature industries are usually those which have levelled out after a growth period. Annual expansion is at the same rate as the general economy. Mature companies usually have an established market niche, traditional cultures, and tend towards conservatism. Staff benefits in such companies are often broad and accessible to everyone. Internal career development is encouraged, and the organisation is highly structured. It could be a good move to join such a company if you are developing your career and need to pursue further education and training, if you are interested in gaining broad experience, or if you recognise the potential of mobility between divisions or in overseas service. If you have entrepreneurial zeal you might be frustrated by the stodginess of management and the lack of acknowledgement for your innovative ideas. You may also feel the hierarchical structure is unwieldy and uncompromising. It really depends on your personality and your ability to break through tradition.

So how do you determine where your targeted company stands in its life cycle? Scour industry magazines, annual reports, general newspaper and magazine articles. Look at their web site and use the Internet to gather further information. Talk to people in the industry and to placement consultants. Plot graphs of the company's profits over the past five years to get a feel for its growth potential and strategies. When you've done that, answer these questions:

- What are the past and future trends of the particular industry?
- What is happening to sales? Do they appear to be increasing, holding their own, or falling off? (For example, tobacco is hardly a growth sector!)
- Is this an industry that is open to substitute products?
- Does this industry have a tendency to diversification?
- What is happening with industry expansion or reduction?
- Is the product one of new technology?
- Is the product one that has attracted newcomers to the field?

When you have generally positioned a company into the birth, growth or mature stage, then list further possible questions you should answer either before an interview, or at the interview:

- What products does the company make and what share of the market does it hold?
- Who are the major competitors, and how are they holding up against this company's strategies?
- What is the company's strategy—cost effectiveness, quality, service? A combination of all three?
- Where does the company stand on technology—is it a leader or a follower?
- Is the company losing market share? If so, what are its diversification plans to change this situation?
- Is there a capital works expansion program in progress? Are new offices/factories being opened?

- How does the company rate with profits over the last five and ten years?
- What strategies are proposed to set this company apart from its competitors in the future?
- Does the company have an international outlook?

These questions may be difficult to answer if your target company is a major corporation with separate divisions. While you should treat those divisions as individual companies, you must do extra homework to get an overview of the entire organisation, because divisions are often constrained by conservative management structures which could influence output in the long run.

UNDERSTANDING THE MARKETPLACE — LARGE COMPANIES VERSUS SMALL COMPANIES

Large versus small is not the same issue it was in the past. As we said earlier, company structures are changing—the hiving off of divisions, new technology and modern management practices are affecting the way large companies operate to the extent that many of them can look like a task force of small companies joined together. However, there are some basic differences and we should discuss them.

Status and visibility in a large company with well-known brand names may be important to you. But don't buy your career choice based on the marketplace image or quality of the brand name, because some of the more challenging careers could well be within an organisation which perhaps hasn't such a high profile but which can offer you, as an individual, a more challenging opportunity. The key here is not to be constrained in your choice by an organisation's image or you may be doing your career a disservice.

Naturally, companies differ in their management structure and in the way they operate. Once you have targeted certain companies, you'll have to research their particular *modus operandi*. There are, however, some generalisations that can be made about careers in large and small organisations. For the purpose of this exercise, big companies are those with at least 1000 employees and a variety of operating facets. Smaller companies are those with less than 1000 employees and may have either one product or many.

Large companies—better training but further from the cutting edge

Narrow job specification

Usually you would enter such organisations in a defined and narrow-function job role, with the promise of being moved to various departments in order to gain general experience of, and exposure to, the organisation. The experience you gain will be deeper and more specialised than it would be in a smaller organisation.

Broad but restricted movement

Large companies will often have broader advancement opportunities with more choice than smaller companies. Also, large corporations with subsidiaries are often able to move employees between companies without loss of staff benefits and superannuation. Don't expect to be rotated as quickly as you might like. Some large companies have a policy requiring at least two to three years in a specific job.

Potential for higher salaries

Company size is often related to salary potential: if you're a manager in a large company you are likely to be paid more of a basic package than if you're a manager in a smaller company where high income can only be paid out for high performance.

More benefits

Large companies usually offer more comprehensive staff benefits such as medical insurance, superannuation, tertiary education reimbursement, staff clubs, canteens and subsidised loans. Although company benefits shouldn't be the main reason you choose a particular organisation, they should be considered when you are looking at remuneration packages.

Training

Larger companies tend to have a bigger budget for training and a more systematic and structured approach. Smaller companies do train, but they rely more heavily on *you the individual* to drive your needs in that area. This is why it was always assumed the training was better in larger companies. It's just more visible—and that's important to many people, particularly those starting their careers.

Smaller companies—close to the action and more autonomy

Broader experience

In small organisations you're likely to get broader-based experience and more responsibility. There are usually closer lines of communication to the boss, so you could be reporting direct to a senior manager.

Greater visibility

The chances are you'll be noticed more often and earlier. In a small company you'll be given the opportunity to affect special projects. Remember, greater responsibility also means greater accountability—your mistakes will also be visible.

Greater potential to influence

Most of your actions in a small company will have some effect on the organisation. The success of your projects can affect the bottom line, whereas in a larger organisation you may just be a cog in the wheel and have no overview of specific projects and their part in company profits. You will experience less objectivity in smaller companies with owners/directors and you will have to put up with this as the other side of the bureaucracy coin.

So don't assume that your only opportunities are with large companies. Smaller and medium-sized companies are now seeing the value of taking on younger, well-qualified people and have more confidence in their ability to bring these people through and expand their knowledge base. It is generally assumed that the growth in new jobs will be faster in smaller to medium-sized companies.

However, some industries are predisposed to large organisations. You can't be a telecommunications carrier unless you are a big company. So if you have your heart set on getting into telecommunications it's important to gear yourself up to working for a big company and develop the appropriate skills.

Where you are involved in networking through a matrix of different skills across a national organisation you'll probably have to develop better facilitation skills. In a small company where you are able to engage in the total business, that's not so important.

CAREER OPPORTUNITIES

Some of the new growth industries are discussed here.

Telecommunications

This is an obvious growth area, particularly in Australia, with deregulation and new carriers and resellers. Just as important are the *spin-offs* we get from telecommunications: personal paging communications companies which, when merged with information technology, provide a seamless information network for individuals and corporations alike; companies which supply hardware or software solutions; consultants to companies on these areas. These spin-offs will all be part of the developing telecommunication industry as we move from the old industrial age, which we called *auto-*mation, to the new *info*-mation age where the transmission and use of information becomes the key to corporate competitiveness in meeting the demands of the consumer.

Recreation and tourism

The biggest non-government employer worldwide is the recreation and tourism industry. The general trend towards working longer hours but with more time off, retiring earlier, and living longer, healthier lives has increased the demand for recreation and leisure activities.

When you consider tourism and leisure in terms of jobs, don't just think of airlines and hotel chains. Think laterally—travel agents, coach companies, duty-free stores, companies that make or clean linen for hotels, courier services, bed & breakfast accommodation, personal pagers, restaurants (take-away and eat-in), diving schools, the entertainment industry—just to name a few!

Health care

Health care continues to be a growth industry. Deregulation, increasing corporatisation of health care, a more proactive approach on the part of the individual towards health care, and an ageing population are all contributing factors to the growth in private sector jobs. We will continue to see an increase in private health service providers and, as the expense of institutionalising people rises, rapid growth in the home-care area: community nursing, meals on wheels, house cleaning, companions for the aged.

Then there is the alternative health care area which will provide huge growth in jobs with the general acceptance of natural therapies such as acupuncture, iridology and osteopathy, which emphasise prevention rather than treatment, and a holistic approach of not just looking at the problem but at the cause of the problem.

With a more health-conscious population we can include peripheral businesses such as weight-loss centres, gyms and gym equipment. In California one company started Dial A Gym. The gym is in the back of a truck which pulls up to your house—complete with personal trainer—ready for your work-out. The business has grown to over 1000 trucks and is a good example of how new industries can grow out of fairly conventional areas.

Remember, from a government's perspective, anything that encourages people to become healthier means big savings in health dollars. So governments will be right behind growth in these preventative areas.

In the area of public health we have seen the outsourcing of various functions to private companies from catering, linen supply, transport and medical product distribution, to the managing of specific elements of the hospital sector. In this area competition will also come from overseas: who can provide the cheapest, most cost-effective hospital bed?

As hospitals take a more holistic view of their expenditure there is a growth area for specialised people—computer programmers, systems people, high technology biomedical people and service technicians—who can maintain the sophisticated technology necessary and monitor the cost of expensive procedures.

Biotechnology is another growth area both here and overseas for specialists in the areas of medical science, physiology and biochemistry, and in ethical issues such as genetic engineering.

Australia is at the forefront of microsurgery, ophthalmic surgery and cardiac surgery. The Federal Government has a program to foster technology development in these and other strong areas of expertise with a view to export markets. There is also export potential in the area of hospital management in terms of administration, purchasing, people management, personnel management and general health care administration.

Financial services

The financial institutions of the future will not just be banks where we borrow or lend money: they will be financial advisory shops which will provide complete solutions to financial planning needs. And you won't even have to leave home—you'll be able to access the service through your phone or television via new telecommunications systems. The product development, marketing and selling process of new banking services will create a demand for a new breed of people not currently employed by many financial institutions.

With an ageing population and a government determined to reduce its budget deficits in relation to pension subsidies through enforced superannuation saving, it is likely that we will continue to see an increase in the amount of money allocated to retirement. This will lead to significant growth in the areas of funds management, investment management and financial planning.

For people who can add value and who can adopt a proactive investment advisory approach to servicing the community's needs, the changes in the financial services field will make it a competitive, exciting and interesting area in which to work.

Manufacturing

In the area of manufacturing we need to take advantage of our natural resources and add value to our products for an overseas market. New jobs will be created only when we refine our raw materials, be they agricultural or mineral, before we export them, rather than letting this process happen overseas. Tuna fish, fruit, cereals, vegetables, fine wool (not greasy wool), iron ore—any commodity that we can dig out of the ground, or grow, or produce, then add some value to before we sell it—will be part of this growth area for manufacturing.

It is hard for Australia to compete with countries that have sophisticated manufacturing industries created by large domestic volumes of production, but we can be entre-preneurial in identifying niche markets where Australia can use some of its natural advantages and add value to the product. Sectors which require a high content of 'tailor-made' manufacturing will also do well as local producers have the advantage in servicing niche markets.

The manufacture of high-technology products continues to be an area of opportunity. The industry relies on high-level skills and manufacturing technology rather than volume and cost of labour.

Resources and mining

Australia's natural resources/mining industries will continue to be a reasonably steady sector of demand, although technology will impact on the total number of jobs per tonne output.

There will be some real opportunities in resources to expand overseas markets for value-added products or niche markets, and any pressure on global energy prices will accentuate this trend. Again, the complexity and quality of the jobs will be such that there will be a need for a multi-skilled, flexible, export-oriented range of executives who are generally more marketing and customer focused than technically biased.

There is an ongoing trend to undertake projects as joint ventures and consortiums. This also allows success in major international markets.

Agriculture

The wine industry provides a good example of value-added agriculture in Australia. The value of grapes compared to the bottle of wine that is made from them and then exported is a ratio of 1:5. Sold as grapes, the income would be one-fifth of what we get by producing a bottle of wine. And because the wine industry has developed its expertise in marketing, Australia is now recognised internationally as a great wine producer.

In agriculture we are beginning to concentrate on marketing. The first step is to identify the need. If there's a market for rice wafers in Indonesia, we grow the rice, manufacture the rice wafers, and ship out the finished product, thereby achieving higher returns.

The cotton industry is another example. Exports of cotton have risen significantly over the last decade. Value added has potential, both in Australia and overseas. We have to think laterally in terms of cotton and wool blends; or boutique spinning—short runs, rather than on the scale of a Bradmill or a Bonds.

PROJECTED EMPLOYMENT GROWTH BY OCCUPATION 1991-2001

TOP TEN		BOTTOM TEN	
1	Social Worker	1	Councellors and ministers of religion
2	Psychologists	2	Agricultural labourers
3	Economists	3	Farmers/farm managers
4	Information Science	4	Air traffic controllers/ship pilots
5	Veterinarians	5	Power chemical plant operators
6	Computing professionals	6	Trades assistants (unskilled workers)
7	Speech pathologists	7	Machine operators
8	Welfare/Youth workers	8	Repair and installation tradespeople
9	Accountants	9	Cleaners
10	Pharmacists	10	Aircraft pilots

Percentage growth

Source: Department of Employment, Education and Training

5 CAREER PATHS BY KEY DISCIPLINES

We have chosen a variety of key disciplines to provide you with a formula for researching your specific area of interest.

Accountancy

One of the advantages of being an accountant is that any organisation which incurs expenses or earns revenue needs to employ an accountant, either on a permanent or part-time consulting basis.

In general, accountants work for employers in two separate and distinct categories: one is commerce and industry, which includes government; the other is public accounting, the firms of chartered accountants or professional accounting firms which sell their services on a 'fee-for-service' basis to the broader community.

Accounting qualifications will vary and are linked to membership of one of the professional accounting bodies. In summary:

- ACA—a member of the Institute of Chartered Accountants;
- CPA—a member of the Australian Society of Practising Accountants;
- NIA—a member of the National Institute of Accountants.

You must be an accounting graduate to gain membership to the ACA and the CPA, whilst a Technical Certificate Course is sufficient to gain entry to the NIA. All three are well recognised, albeit the first two more so than the NIA qualification. There's also a UK qualification which is becoming more predominant in Australia—the Chartered Institute of Management Accountants (CIMA), which is primarily a specialist management/manufacturing accounting-based qualification.

A fundamental shift in the nature of accounting occurred in the 1980s and the 1990s. Financial accounting, which focused on processing and recording historical financial information, became less labour intensive as a result of more advanced technology. Accordingly, there was a transfer of resources to management accounting. The latter, which focuses on analysing and forecasting business performance, has grown in prominence as the mainstay of accounting in commerce, industry and government.

The financial accountant is responsible for processing and recording financial transactions, and ensuring that historical statutory accounts comply with accounting standards and the *Companies Act,* whereas the management accountant is responsible for using the data created by the financial accountant as the basis for interpreting current financial results and forecasting future business performance.

The management accountant is more integrated into the operations of the business: assisting in the development of business strategies; measuring performance; working with sales and marketing personnel to analyse product performance; searching out reasons behind achievement or non-achievement of budgets.

Apart from this fundamental shift in the nature of accounting, there has also been a significant shift in the type of accounting being conducted within the different industry sectors. For instance:

- in *government,* basic cash accounting principles have been upgraded to incorporate more sophisticated, accrual-based accounting, where relevant expenses and revenues are allocated to the period to which they relate, versus the period in which they are incurred.
- in *public accounting,* or the 'Profession' as it is called, technology has precipitated major changes. For instance, systems-based audits which analyse and measure risk have replaced the old compliance-based audits, significantly reducing the human resources required. Public accounting is broadening its base from straightforward accounting, tax and audit to encompass other services: insolvency; information technology and human resources consulting; corporate advisory services and more generalist management consultancies.

Traditional corporate ladder scenario

Chartered accounting can mean working in a one-person suburban office or a large international partnership employing hundreds of staff, so obviously opportunities to move up the ladder vary from company to company. Generally you progress from graduate to senior accountant, supervisor and then manager. The ultimate aim would be to achieve equity in the business as a partner.

In the *commercial sector* you would normally progress through financial accounting and management accounting to the role of a Financial Controller. In a large organisation the next level is Finance Director. All accounting and administration areas report to the Finance Director, who sometimes assumes broader responsibility in the areas of distribution, logistics and warehousing.

A new position title has emerged: Commercial Manager or Commercial Director. This person works closely with the Chief Executive or General Manager in developing strategies and has responsibility for most aspects of the business other than sales and marketing.

As an *alternative to accounting* you might consider the financial services sector: non-accounting areas in banking such as capital markets, foreign exchange, corporate lending, corporate advisory and financial planning, which uses your knowledge to sell superannuation and investments schemes.

Accountants can also use their numeric skills effectively in the following fields:

- general management—with a service industry or one where specific industry experience is unnecessary;
- management consulting—to a variety of organisations;
- selling software, financial products, or financial packages in the computer industry;
- lecturing at universities, colleges, schools, colleges of advanced education;
- owning your own business (where financial skills are important);
- recruitment consultancy with specialist firms;
- company secretary, particularly becoming involved with the statutory aspects of a company;

- administrators or chief executives of cooperatives, banks, legal firms, chartered accountancy firms, charitable organisations and non-profit organisations;
- stockbroking, particularly analysis work or client advisory roles.

Advertising

An advertising agency can be a large multinational or a three-person band, offering full service or outsourcing both media and creative areas. In some agencies, the creative division rules the roost. Others are more strategically or account-service based.

There are three distinct career paths: creative, media, and account service—the latter being the linchpin between the client and the other two.

Traditional corporate ladder scenario

Account service: Account Executive, Account Manager, Account Director, Group Account Director, then General Manager or Managing Director—depending on the size. A leaner structure might not have all these levels. For example, a good Account Director will sometimes go straight through to Managing Director.

Media: Media Assistant, Media Planner/Buyer, Group Head, Media Manager, and finally Media Director, who reports through to the Managing Director.

Creative: It is usual for an art director and a copywriter to work in a team. Once established, this partnership will often move as a team to other agencies. The Creative Director heads this section, which often incorporates the production department.

Today advertising has a much leaner structure. There is not a big intake and the industry is more sophisticated in its recruitment and the level of people employed, in terms of skills and qualifications.

An effective way for a young person to gain entry into advertising is through the Graduate Training Program, run by the Advertising Federation of Australia (AFA). The nine-month course is designed to give hands-on experience across all the sectors within an advertising agency. For those who wish to specialise in a creative discipline, the Australian Writers and Art Directors Association (AWARD) run a short part-time course.

Another way in is from the client side, making the transition from assistant product manager, product manager or marketing manager in a consumer packaged goods company, such as Johnson & Johnson, to accounts manager or account director. This is an ideal background as it also enables you to cross back to the client side.

Advertising agencies are very approachable and are passionate about their industry. If you want a job in the business, get to know how it functions. Carry out research—read the trade journals, talk to people, be aware of which agencies are doing what, understand *why* you want to work in this industry.

Advertising is a communication industry that requires someone who thinks on their feet laterally, strategically—or both; who can be diplomatic yet assertive; who is a good negotiator; who has the ability to impress, sell an idea, influence, motivate and develop relationships with clients and colleagues. You're also at the client's beck and call, so be prepared to work long hours.

The big salaries—especially for creative personnel—are offset by poor job security. If the agency loses an account, you could lose your job. There's a lot of movement between agencies, not necessarily for more money, but often for a better career path, more job security or a better title.

Another big change is occurring where agencies are becoming multi-skilled, incorporating communication arms—public relations, sales promotion, direct marketing—to provide a total communications solution for their customers. Career options could be:

- making the transition to the client side, perhaps in a product or marketing management role;
- pursuing a career in sales promotion, direct response marketing, or public relations;
- starting your own agency—the eventual goal of a lot of creative and account service people;
- working freelance—particularly in creative areas;
- if your experience has been gained in media you might make a move into television; manage a communications arm of a marketing group; or move to a media-buying shop.

Financial services

In financial services there is a move away from traditional areas towards a more service-oriented industry. Banks (wholesale and retail), building societies, stockbrokers, insurance companies and fund managers have become distribution networks for a product which basically revolves around money: personal loans, mortgages, credit cards, shares, superannuation, corporate lending, government project funding, equity under-writing and money market and currency trading.

The funds management area is a huge growth market for jobs, from managerial and marketing, to development of products designed to meet changing investor requirements. The ability to deliver an effective product and service is a prime praxis for all the financial services area.

In the banking industry particularly, as the demand for borrowing declines, there has been a huge shift towards the funds management area with a growth area for jobs around the service enhancements that banks (both wholesale and retail) are pushing in their scramble for market share.

Banking

The banking industry comprises two markets: *wholesale* and *retail*. Each has a distinct market focus with very different career paths.

The wholesale banking industry—all merchant and investment banks—has four main streams:

- treasury and capital markets—the money market and foreign exchange area;
- corporate funding—business finance and providing debt to corporate and institutional clients (including government);
- corporate advisory—strategic advice to corporations in areas such as mergers, acquisitions, takeovers, public issues and underwriting;
- wholesale funds management—this area requires a knowledge of how the money market works and strategic investment in order to enhance returns on large portfolios of money such as companies' superannuation.

Wholesale banking and wholesale funds management generally require a tertiary education. A degree could be in economics, law, commerce, or science for some of the more quantitative roles. A mathematical drive is compatible with an environment that deals with money, complex products and formulas. Graduates are expected to become income-generating early in their careers. They move fairly quickly up a responsibility curve, sometimes reaching management levels within ten years and earning upwards of $150 000. The earning potential in this area is probably higher than in any other industry.

Retail banking has moved away from the traditional teller and information desk to be more service-driven in focus.

While a job in retail banking doesn't necessarily require a tertiary qualification, these days, graduates—in, for example, the fields of commerce and economics—are employed for career-stream jobs.

Human resources

Human resources continues to be a significant growth area. There is a simple reason: corporations recognise that people are their greatest asset and they are utilising more staff— either external consultants or adding to their human resources department—with skills in performance management and strategic development to assist in improving productivity through their personnel. There will, therefore, be an increase in the use of contemporary behavioural practices to improve the way organisations hire people, train people, develop people, pay people, and if they don't meet the current skill requirements of the organisation, work out ways of fixing that problem, rather than condoning non-performance.

Information technology (IT)

The rate of technological innovation has moved more rapidly in the last three years than in any other previous period and will continue to do so as we move closer to the new millenium. Technology has driven change in all areas of business and in all business arenas—vendor, banking and finance, consumer, industrial, retail, hospitality, travel, etc. The favourite and most exciting development in IT has been the growth of the Internet. Web development, multimedia, intranets and extranets have brought a new dimension to the storage and retrieval of information.

IT job numbers have increased in many areas such as ERP implementations, systems upgrades and Year 2000 projects. The skills required in these areas can be very specific and include the need for technical certification. Specialised product knowledge such as SAP or Oracle expertise are areas of high demand and high return in salary. The advent of outsourcing and facilities management organisations has brought volume demand to the industry but has reduced the number of IT staff directly employed in some of the larger public and private organisations.

One of the most significant changes in the recruitment of IT is the emphasis that is now placed on the personal attributes of potential employees. IT is no longer a back-room function. Most roles are now very business oriented and require extensive liaison with customers at all levels—internal and external. Verbal and written communication skills, sometimes specific industry knowledge, tertiary qualifications, positive references from previous employers, leadership and influencing skills and, of course, technical capability, are all attributes that are sought in candidates.

However, the sought-after IT candidate can also be as selective as the prospective employer. Researching an organisation through the Internet and providing detailed job descriptions are essential. Career opportunity, professional working environment, support of technology by the business functions and ownership of projects by business sponsors are specific requirements by senior and talented employees. The move to global organisations which offer international travel is also having a marked effect on the industry.

Law

Financial deregulation, heightened stockmarket activity and an enormous property boom generated extraordinary growth in the legal profession during the 1980s. Australia's law firms grew—some almost trebled in size—in disproportion to the economy. As the property market deflated, along with the big entrepreneurs, much legal work disappeared overnight, never to be replaced.

In the 1990s the market matured, if not contracted. Growth in business will now come from some new areas, but the bulk comes from taking work away from competitors. There is a greater level of uncertainty about the future and the glamour of the big money has dissolved—salaries, from those of graduates to partners, have contracted.

Increased competition is also coming from in-house counsel and from outside the legal profession in the shape of merchant bankers, business advisers, investment advisers, management consultants, industrial-relations consultants, and particularly accountants (where some of the large international firms have set up their own legal arms). The merging of an accountancy firm with a law firm to provide business services is a reasonable prospect for the future.

Clients want solutions to their problems, not just legal advice, and law firms need to look at these broader areas as well as the technical side. The main challenge for law firms now is to run as a lean, efficient, productivity-based business. Many run internal management training programs for staff, and some have even hired external General Managers or Operations Managers to run their businesses.

Technical skills are taken for granted. Employers are interested in value-adding skills: an ability to train people, supervise and delegate effectively; marketing skills; managerial skills; strategic planning skills; financial skills; public speaking skills; and *the key factor—an ability to create and sustain relationships with clients.*

Traditional career path scenario

The traditional career path is graduate solicitor, solicitor, senior solicitor, associate, senior associate (where you are given the status of your name on the letterhead), and—the ultimate goal for most lawyers—partner. A partner is a combination shareholder/director and self-employed person.

At graduate level, look at developing interpersonal skills. You might start off with a double degree in, say, Science, Economics, or Arts, or work in a legal aid centre dealing with people. Get some experience whilst you are studying. If you're further down the track with law as a second degree you're ahead of the game. The more exposure you can get, the greater your prospects for employment.

Familiarise yourself with the law in the early stages of your career. Which broad area interests you? Which core specialities?

For a solicitor, there are two main avenues: litigation (going to court), or transactional (not going to court), and within those two very broad divisions there are a range of other options. These include, for example:

- corporate, commercial and taxation law, which covers areas such as trade practices, mergers and acquisitions, industrial and intellectual property and capital gains tax;
- employment and industrial relations law, which covers discrimination and unfair dismissal, industrial disputes, affirmative action, redundancy packages and retrenchment procedures;
- banking and finance, which covers areas such as trade practices, problem management, insolvency, funds management, project finance, finance litigation;
- environment and planning law, which deals with such areas as government policies, development and building, natural resources and pollution control.

Areas such as environmental law, intellectual property, industrial relations and superannuation are growth areas because of the complexity of the government regulations that surround them.

There is also a move towards exporting Australian legal services to the Asian-Pacific region.

In the future law firms will have to look at more inventive ways to stay afloat. Contract work is a real possibility, where the need will be for multi-skilled people who can turn their hand from mergers and acquisitions to bankruptcy and consultancy; from litigation to transactional work. Part-time partners and job-sharing are also options for the future.

If you're thinking of a lateral career move you might look at becoming in-house counsel for a corporation; joining an accounting practice; going into government or politics; becoming a strategic business adviser to major corporations; becoming a lobbyist; or perhaps making a move into management within a law firm.

Marketing

Marketing covers a number of different areas:

- *consumer*—for example, fast-moving packaged goods companies such as Johnson & Johnson or Colgate Palmolive, as well as companies providing consumer durables such as Panasonic or Sunbeam;
- *industrial*—for example, BHP;
- *service*—for example, a merchant or retail bank; the hospitality and travel industries.

Very few positions are available to you without tertiary qualifications: traditionally a Bachelor of Commerce or a Bachelor of Business with a marketing major, or for some companies a broader degree in Arts or Economics with an emphasis on Communications. In the future, in addition to your marketing degree you might have an MBA or a Masters degree.

Traditional corporate ladder scenario

The traditional corporate ladder scenario is to begin as a marketing trainee or sales representative with a view to becoming an assistant product manager for two years; product manager for three to four years; group product manager; marketing manager; marketing and sales director (sometimes two separate positions); general manager or managing director.

An ideal entry point would be as a marketing trainee in a blue-chip consumer packaged goods company, where you would progress to product manager. In this environment you have exposure to all elements of the marketing mix: advertising, public relations, sales promotion, market research, marketing plans, forecasting sales, and pricing. Promotion *within* the company further testifies to your ability. This experience gives you a choice of a number of different career options:

- progress further within the current organisation to marketing manager;
- gain experience on the sales side in your current organisation, possibly as sales manager/national account manager/State manager. It is important to have experience in both marketing and sales if your goal is to work through to general management;
- move to an advertising agency working on high-volume packaged goods accounts where your strategic marketing experience will be useful in the development of advertising and creative strategies;
- a career in banking, financial services or insurance where your packaged goods marketing skills—strong strategic thinking, interpersonal and communication skills—and exposure to the marketing mix are highly sought after;
- the accounting and law disciplines are still behind the consumer goods area in terms of acceptance and implementation of marketing but they are growth areas. To remain competitive, these industries have seen the need to be more marketing-oriented;

- a more entrepreneurial hands-on marketing environment such as the publishing or media industry, that will provide further diversity in general marketing experience;
- one of the communications spheres, such as sales promotion, public relations or direct-response marketing; or perhaps a strategic specialist area such as management consulting.

Marketing is a growth area. In leaner times, increasing competition has led to its recognition as a necessary tool to sell the product.

Sales

In the past, *sales representatives* and *account managers* were associated only with retail, the grocery industry, or those companies selling products directly to the public. But sales skill is in demand in all sectors of our community and is readily transferable across most industries. Today everyone wants a good salesperson! Government organisations are even employing those with sales skills to meet the needs of their internal or external customers.

To build or broaden your career, consider obtaining experience in people management, and in managing a sales budget within your industry.

As a *senior or middle level sales manager* you will now have experience in people management as well as sales and negotiation. You will also have extensive experience in your own particular industry. Consider a move towards national sales management which gives you both broader responsibility and input at a more strategic level of the business. Consulting to your industry in various fields would also be an option: consider personnel consulting, strategy consulting, or running your own brokerage/agency to perform a sales service for manufacturers.

HOW TO GET INFORMATION

Talk to everyone in your targeted industry and, if possible, your chosen organisation. There will always be someone who knows someone! Ask your friends, family or a consultant. As well as reading industry publications to get a feel for the movers and shakers in your chosen field, seek out your chosen company's *annual report* and *company brochures* to understand specific details of its functions and operations. Look at *industry directories* such as the *Directory of Australian Book Publishers,* or *The Hospitals and Health Services Yearbook;* these cover many of the smaller firms not listed in business directories. Ask your contact in the industry for information, or check the library.

Business and trade publications keep you abreast of trends in your industry, alert you to opportunities and to economic and political events which could have an impact on the operations of your potential employer. *Professional association publications* often provide valuable information about industry trends and current developments; they also advertise jobs. Keep relevant articles to refresh your memory and to give you that extra ammunition before any direct communication. A name mentioned in an article can enable you to personalise your calls and letters.

Use the Internet. The Internet is not only fast and international but can lead you to further information sources.

Reference sources

The State Library has a Reference and Information Centre. A business services librarian is available during normal hours.

The library has a number of valuable business information references covering details such as ownership of a company, foreign operations, subsidiaries, net worth and profit, key personnel: *Jobson's Year Book of Public Companies*; *Kompass Australia—Volumes 1 and 2*; *The Corporate Handbook*; *The Business Who's Who of Australia*; *The Financial Services Directory*; *Directory of Australian Associations*; *Australian Public Affairs Information Service (APAIS)*; *Commonwealth Government Gazette*; *Australia's Top 500 Companies*; *The Australian Key Business Directory*; *The Stock Exchange Research Handbook*.

Your local library has reference books, audio visual material, current local, interstate and overseas newspapers, and a variety of journals and magazines. Computers, word processors and photocopiers are also available for public use.

The Australian Institute of Management (AIM) has a specialist reference library in some States. AIM also runs numerous management-related courses—contact them for a brochure.

The Australian Securities Commission has information on all companies registered in Australia and will do a company search for a small fee.

The Australian Stock Exchange has excellent company research facilities which are open to the public for a fee. It also offers a Limited Company Review Service which comprises a report on every listed company based on its Annual Report and the official records received by the Stock Exchange.

The Small Business office of the State Government fulfils an advisory role and can assist intending and existing small business owners with the aid of an extensive range of services and packages.

The local *Chamber of Commerce* represents business in each area and can provide valuable contacts.

The Chamber of Manufactures, NSW, has an information and referral centre run by a librarian and deals with a range of data relating to industrial relations, economics, management and business management.

Other sources of useful information include the Commonwealth Government Bookshop; the State Government Bookshop; Professional Employment Services and agencies; and Morgan & Banks Pty Ltd.

The phone book

The telephone book is one of the most up-to-date reference listings and a valuable tool if used properly. For instance, if you're targeting specific industries, the *Yellow Pages* will give you your first checklist of companies. The key is to approach the perimeter of your target market for information *before* you attack the more prominent companies.

Ask for the person responsible for employment (small firms often don't have a personnel department), or the manager or general manager. You might say you've heard about the growth of, for example, the food manufacturing business and could they tell you:

- which companies are doing well;
- why they are doing well;
- what contributes to their success;
- what sort of market share they have;
- whether they are locally or foreign owned;
- the appropriate person to speak to in those organisations in terms of employment;
- what the career opportunities are.

People are very helpful if approached in the right way. Use a telephone script if it gives you an edge. *(See* Step 6, Packaging Your Assets.)

A useful technique is to photocopy the relevant page of the *Yellow Pages*. Have an appropriate column marked as to whom you have spoken to on the phone and the necessary follow-up action. Start at A and even if there are 100 names in that industry group, only stop when you have achieved your goal.

HOW TO UTILISE CONTACTS

People have tried to put a percentage on it, but let's say more than 50 per cent of positions tend to go to people through an informal network as opposed to those being aggressively advertised or given to search consultants.

A lot of job opportunities are never advertised. Many potential employers are not even aware that they may be able to utilise your skills and abilities in their business. This hidden job market can often only be accessed through networking.

Networking is, for most people, the most powerful technique available for conducting a job search. It helps produce a list of people from whom to get information and ideas, and ultimately it should produce a contact list which becomes a major part of the job search.

SO HOW DO YOU TAKE ADVANTAGE OF IT?

- Start with your diary, list everyone you have had lunch with in the last three years and everyone you thought worth recording at the time.
- List your suppliers, customers, and co-workers—past and present.

- List other professionals in your field.
- List personal contacts—friends and casual acquaintances.
- List family contacts—go back to the third cousin on your partner's side.
- List your neighbours—opposite and either side of you; who do *they* know?
- List your accountant, lawyer, doctor, dentist and local chamber of commerce representative.
- List your old lecturer at university or high school teacher.
- List the people talking to you on the touchline when you are watching your children play sport on Saturday morning.

Contacts are worth a great deal and should be cultivated accordingly. Seize every opportunity. The depth and breadth of all our personal networks is huge when we stop to think about it.

If your next-door neighbour is in electronics, ask how the electronics industry is going. If the parent of one of your kids' best friends is a banker, ask what's going on in the financial services sector. If you used to work for an industrial marketing company, many of your customers were in the distribution business—maybe one of those organisations has an interesting job that might suit you down to the ground?

Make yourself visible socially and businesswise. Attend conferences, seminars, conventions and trade shows around your chosen industry. Most of your potential employers will probably be there—or, at the very least, some new contacts. Don't neglect peripheral conferences such as Human Resources or Business and the Environment. At the end of the conference you are usually given a print-out of the name, title and organisation of everyone who attended—a ready-made contact list. Check the paper or industry magazines for details. If you're unemployed, this will help keep you in touch with the latest developments in your field.

Maintain memberships with professional organisations. By doing this you keep in contact with your industry and the people in it.

Some background principles

The best way of making new contacts is working on your old contacts. You don't ring them up and say, 'I'm looking for a job or a career.' You ring them up for advice about their area of expertise: 'Who do you know, because I'm interested in XYZ?' 'Who do you know who may know someone in XYZ company?' Or you can develop opportunities randomly: 'I'm looking for a role (selling fast-moving consumer goods): who do you think I should be talking to?'

When you get a referral, be sure to ask if you can use your contact's name as an introduction.

When you suggest to someone that they can assist you, there is only one chance in three that they will immediately think of how they can do this. Therefore, follow-up on your part is essential.

The networking approach

This approach should be utilised in contacting senior people in a particular field or organisation (someone who could, possibly, have the authority either to hire you or to influence such a decision). By the time you get to this stage you will know everything about the company, such as its products, services, subsidiaries, problem areas, and the role the person you are contacting has within the organisation. You know all this because you have thoroughly researched these areas.

Remember, you are not necessarily looking for a specific job: you are only interested in exploring the opportunities available to someone with your abilities, skills and background in this industry or organisation. You need to be very clear about this. (You will, of course, consider any job offers, but at this stage you are just interested in researching the marketplace.) Aim to generate at least two additional leads from each telephone call.

Your telephone approach

Remember, when speaking on the telephone, to *smile* and always use your source as an introduction.

> *Contact* John Jones.
> *You* Hello, John, this is Roger Smart. I am wondering if you can help me. Elizabeth Jenkins suggested I give you a call. I am looking at ongoing career prospects in the (fast-moving consumer goods area) and Elizabeth thought that you may be able to give me some advice, which I'd certainly appreciate. Could we get together for say twenty minutes?

HERE ARE SOME POSSIBLE OUTCOMES:

> *Contact* I'm not sure that I'm the right person.
> *You* Well, anything would help, but if that's the case, perhaps you can refer me to someone else.

> *Contact* You're looking for a job.
> *You* Perhaps eventually. But I need to do some more research first.

> *Contact* Sure.
> *You* Great. What's a suitable time for you?

Some people may find it more appropriate to make initial contact via a letter. The content should follow the same lines as the telephone approach and indicate when you will call to arrange an appointment.

Your meeting

Before you leave home to go to your meeting you need to be clear about your purpose and have an established agenda. Your purpose is to:

- gather or confirm information about the company and industry;
- discuss your skills and background and where they might contribute to the company or industry;
- get two more contact names.

YOUR AGENDA COULD COVER:

- arriving early to read or pick-up any information available about the company at reception;
- a few minutes of friendly chat at the beginning of the meeting to build rapport;
- checking the time your contact has available to talk to you;
- asking open-ended questions about the company or industry;
- giving a brief summary of your own skills, qualifications and experience;
- asking for advice on where you might fit in the industry or confirming your own ideas;
- asking who else in the industry you could contact;
- thanking your contact and assuring them you will keep them informed about how you get on.

After the meeting, carefully record the information you gathered and think through your approach to the suggested contacts.

One last thing: follow-up with a thank-you note and, if you think it is appropriate, a copy of your résumé.

Other tips for networkers

If you are currently working always carry your own business card. If you are unemployed, splurge out and have personal cards printed. It looks professional.

Always carry a pen and something to write on. You never know when a great idea might strike you.

Make sure every contact knows how to get in touch with you. If you don't make it easy for them, they'll give up. Attach your business card to a follow-up thank-you note.

Use prompts and make notes of your conversation; it can give you an opening line. Was this person a source for information on fast the food industry or someone who advertised a vacancy? If so which paper and what date? Keep a copy of the advertisement with your notes. Perhaps it was a referral from your old university professor, or the person you were apprenticed to.

Keeping records of all your contacts is essential. You might have 50–60 calls and letters out there from your three-week job search. You must be able to immediately refer to a system detailing company name and date; which letter you wrote; the name of the person who referred you *(See* Step 3, Capitalising On Your Assets.)

Advertise yourself. *(See* Step 5, Finding a Buyer.) Also consider voluntary work, temporary work or contract work—all these provide opportunities to make contacts.

Networking is also a great way to hone your research skills. And when you get the job, keep adding to your contact book—you never know when it might come in handy.

TARGETING YOUR SPECIFIC JOB

You've gone through the process of self-analysis; your package is tied up in terms of the skills (competencies) you will bring to the organisation, and you've given some thought to the kind of work you want to do—now it's time to find a buyer.

This part of the process involves a number of options whereby you target different organisations which might be interested in the value you would bring to them.

As you will see, this means targeting specific industries— either through a recruitment organisation or directly—to ascertain just what are the job specifications in particular advertisements, and to persuade recruitment companies to act on your behalf.

TARGETING SPECIFIC INDUSTRIES

In this situation you are targeting a specific industry, or a specific discipline such as marketing or accounting. There are two ways to go about this:

- you can approach the organisation directly;
- you can select various professional recruitment consultants and talk to them about your chosen career and which companies you should target.

Targeting specific industries through a recruitment company

Recruitment consultants may well have contacts with a number of relevant companies—their client companies—to whom they can speak directly on your behalf. So before you approach a company yourself you should talk to some professional consultants, see which companies they represent, and what sort of effort they are prepared to make on your behalf. If this comes to nothing, you can still proceed on your own. The logic is that if a consultant sends you as a good-quality candidate to a company they know well, it is better than you approaching the situation cold and having to 'sing' your own praises.

To find out who the specialist recruiter is for your chosen industry:

- check the newspaper to see which companies most typically have the jobs you are seeking;
- when you are in the process of ringing a company direct, ask which recruitment firm they use or would recommend as being a specialist in the area.

If you phone a handful of people and ask the right questions you will soon be on the right track. And the recruitment consultant will be impressed that you have been referred by companies which pay the consultant's fees.

Once you have seen a select group of recruitment companies, and you have decided which one you want to promote you, it's vital to make the others fully aware that you do not want them to make any approaches to companies on your behalf *without your prior approval*. You and the selected recruitment company will then prepare a strategy for marketing you to the organisation that you and the consultants have selected.

Targeting specific industries directly

Make sure you say something specific in your covering letter or phone call to express why you are interested in working there. This should be based on some *thorough research—* don't make a fool of yourself by saying 'I really want to work in your industry because it's a growth area' when in fact, although it looks like a growing industry, it's actually in a 3 per cent decline. This will certainly negate your chances of working with the company.

Be prepared with one or two specific reasons why you are *personally* interested in working in that industry. These should be related to your motivation and your skills or training: 'My father was in the pharmaceutical industry for years and that's where I developed my interest in it. I have recently finished a course in pharmacology.'

If you want to change careers the same thing applies. For instance, you might want to swap from the computer industry to another technical industry and you have an aptitude for systems and numbers. Use that as part of your pitch to the organisation.

INTERPRETING JOB SPECIFICATIONS IN ADVERTISEMENTS

This is an exercise in understanding how newspaper ads are written and what the company is really looking for.

Executive search firms put a lot of effort into enticing candidates to apply for jobs. They're looking for the best available in the field and they have to get it right the first time. From the employer's point of view, the cost of replacing a new member of the company can run to twice their yearly salary, so mistakes are not looked on too kindly.

Pick up Saturday's paper and scour all the boxed ads throughout the main section of the paper. Some are quite creative in appealing to the high-flyer's ego and remuneration demands, as demonstrated by the advertisment on the following page.

This is what's known as *the job and person specification*. It will be the yardstick by which the new employee will be measured. In this case it was written by a recruitment consultant, but it could just as easily have been produced by a personnel officer or departmental manager looking for the right candidate.

But what does it really mean? How should you interpret what this ad is looking for? Let's go through the main reasons why this advertisement was written as it was. What will attract a potential candidate are the hooks. For instance, one hook will always be the package. Does it, at first sight, meet the candidate's requirements?

It's no good thinking that if you say you'll work for less than offered, you might get the job. You must believe in

---

EXCEPTIONAL CONSUMER MARKETING CHALLENGE
$100 000 PACKAGE

Sales Director Potential—Fast-moving Grocery Products Dynamic International Corporation

Salary Is No Object!

This is an exciting new opportunity to build on an established and rapidly expanding business with one of Australia's most dynamic blue-chip companies. It is a profit-centred role and will appeal to a sales-oriented manager who can identify and capitalise on market opportunities. This will involve assessing clients' needs, recommending and justifying leading-edge materials, handling management systems as well as successful project management.

You will probably have at least 10 years marketing experience with relevant technical or project management skills and a proven track record in solution selling. The ability to grow a profitable business and move to more senior management is considered essential.

---

what you're worth and not settle for less (unless, of course, you have an inflated image of yourself or the market rate for a particular job).

Look at the hooks that define the company size and make-up. The clues in this particular ad are in the words *blue chip*, meaning it's a recognised company in its growth or maturity stage; *dynamic* and *capitalise on market opportunities* suggest there is plenty of room for expansion and the culture of the company is not conservative. The role is multifaceted in that the company is not only looking for a person to *manage projects* but also to *manage systems*.

Most importantly, the job involves selling on a broad basis—indicated by *sales-oriented manager* and *a proven track record in solution selling*. While you may not currently be a manager, it's obvious this company is looking for *someone with management potential*—this subtle difference is important. Lastly, an executive selection firm has been appointed which indicates that the company is established and the job is crucial to their operations.

Now look at your own background. Are there any elements in the job that your skills/experience won't satisfy? Is the company looking for graduates? Is it important to be a high-level manager? From the specification it appears that these are not important elements. Are they looking for self-starters? Do they want proactive thinkers? From key words such as *assessing clients' needs, recommending and justifying*, it would seem these are vital components of the job.

Now, what are the pegs on which you can hang your application? If you have *a proven track record in solution selling* you're nearly there. If you have documentation proving your success in *project management* it would appear the job was designed specifically for you.

So you think you fit all the criteria? Before rushing off to write your application, you must ask yourself more personal questions. *In your eyes you might be ideal for the job but, from your interpretation, does the job seem right for you?* While you may have spent the bulk of your career in selling, are you happy to continue in this stream or do you believe it's time for a career change? Just because most of your experience is in a particular area, you shouldn't think this is the only path you can follow. *Employees in all the key disciplines have the capacity to move laterally if only they can see the potential in other careers.*

Let's look at another example:

MANAGING DIRECTOR

Highly Attractive Package
Joint Venture
Instrumentation and Controls

This is a challenging position with a major Australian Public company. The Managing Director will have full responsibility for the overall management of a joint venture operation between two medium-sized Instrumentation and Control companies.

The Managing Director will report directly to the Joint Venture Board and will be an individual who has already held a senior executive role with an engineering or instrumentation organisation. The person will be dedicated and committed to achieving predetermined profit and development objectives.

The responsibility for the management of the company will be through a strong management team (predominantly engineers) directly managing functions covering marketing, sales, finance engineering and materials management.

Traditionally, the company has operated autonomously and it is envisaged that this approach will very definitely match the new management style.

The successful candidate will preferably hold tertiary qualifications in an engineering discipline, and be able to demonstrate a successful track record in achieving results through effective planning, financial control, people management and marketing strategies.

The first clue to the managing director's position is that the company does not specify a salary package. If this is an important role this does not mean that the salary package is lousy, but that they don't want to limit themselves in any way. If they were to put in, say, $150 000, it might frighten off a good young achiever at $100 000, or indeed it might not seem enough for someone who is outstanding, currently earning $150 000, and wanting to move only for an increase on that figure.

Next comes *joint venture*, which suggests that there is possibly an Australian and overseas element involved here. *The subheading* tells you what sort of business they're in, which suggests they are either looking for someone with exposure to that industry or—*and this is where people often disqualify themselves*—no exposure but an avid or keen interest in getting into it. If you haven't been in instrumentation and controls, but can demonstrate that you have been in a similar industry where the key issues such as technology and contracting are involved, then you could still be in with a chance.

If we look more closely, we find *there is a very big clue in the second paragraph* regarding the MD reporting directly to the joint venture board. They want a senior executive with an engineering or instrumentation organisation, but the clue regarding reporting to a joint venture board suggests that they need someone with the diplomacy and cunning to handle what appears to be in effect two bosses from separate companies with possibly slightly different objectives. Therefore, if there was anything in the candidate's background suggesting *a similar previous position,* either working for another joint venture or perhaps having had to report simultaneously to a functional and operational head, this could give the candidate a significant advantage.

Ask yourself: did you register that point; would you notice it; and more importantly, would you use it to your advantage in the letter attached to your résumé and in your interview?

What about the phrase *dedicated and committed to achieving predetermined profit and development objectives*? In plain English that means: *can you get the job done?* and *have you done it before?* Here is an opportunity to talk about the 'runs on the board' that you've had in the past.

Next comes a comment on *team leadership*—getting results through other people. This is a chance to talk about your experience in that area, particularly with multi-disciplinary teams, such as the marketing, sales and finance mentioned. If you've been in engineering, did you have responsibility for developing new business and finance and administration, as well as dealing with the technical area?

Finally the ad says *preferably hold tertiary qualifications in an engineering discipline*—but it's not essential. If you have a commerce or accounting background, but for some reason have been associated with a hi-tech or engineering-oriented company, that would not preclude you from this position in their opinion. Remember the company is keeping its options open because they're looking for the best available person.

On the opposite page is another advertisement for analysis placed in a national paper.

In advertisements such as these there is even greater room for interpretation. They present an ideal opportunity for you to consider your own background in relation to what they are looking for. If you can 'tick off' at least six or seven out of ten of the requirements listed you are a potential candidate for the role.

Here the words *Administration & Benefits* immediately give you the clue that they are looking for someone unusual. The first line of the advertisement reiterates that point. The advertisement is obviously struggling to outline a role that doesn't have an easy-to-relate title. This is a *classic 'describe the driver and not the car' style of advertisement,* which means they are going to talk about the sort of person you are and what you are doing, rather than give the job a simple title. The institution is obviously a bank or an insurance

ADMINISTRATION & BENEFITS EXECUTIVE

Leading Financial Institution
Package around $60 000
+ Performance-related incentives

This is not a run-of-the-mill compensation role.

The position will be filled by a person having special attributes, including management potential and the urge to participate in the activities of an outstanding organisation.

The position, available due to promotion, provides a vital service to the executives of the group in relation to remuneration and a variety of related issues. It demands discussion, advice, strong initiative and a clear understanding of individual needs. The group is not only a leader in its field, enjoying consistent growth and profitability, but also has a reputation for looking after its people and their career development.

Suitable candidates could come from a variety of backgrounds, but the perfect ingredients for this role are:

- A sensitive, open and balanced personality.
- Good listening, communication and analytical skills.
- Relevant exposure to remuneration, FBT and employee benefit issues.
- An interest in a career in Banking Administration with development potential.

If you feel you qualify for this challenging role, then we would like to hear from you. Flexible and attractive remuneration will be negotiated around the above figure to secure the right candidate for this important and high-profile role.

company with a good reputation, and the package, though mentioned specifically at $60 000, has performance-related incentives which means for $60 000 you could reach $70 000, $80 000 or even $100 000, depending on the company.

The desirable *special attributes—management potential and the urge to participate in the activities of an outstanding organisation*—are interesting. That fits almost everyone, so at this stage you're on a winning streak. Because the position is *available as a result of promotion* you know the previous incumbent did not fail, and the specification indicates that the job provides *a vital service to executives of the group in relation to remuneration and other issues.* In other words, this person is primarily responsible for keeping everybody happy in the area of compensation and benefits. Sounds similar to personnel in a way, doesn't it? This position calls for a good communicator to discuss, advise and take strong initiatives, and you could be working in almost any situation.

The real screeners in this ad come when they describe *personal qualities.* Being *sensitive* and *an open and balanced personality* is somewhat unusual. This basically means that if you could honestly describe yourself as someone who was well liked, intuitive, and the sort of person who didn't need to be told twice what someone else was either thinking or feeling, then you could be a candidate for the role. Now you just have to prove it. Any relevant exposure to remuneration or fringe benefits tax and other employee benefit issues is important—this means the candidate could come from legal, tax or accounting backgrounds, as well as personnel.

Re-read these advertisements and superimpose your own background on them, just for the exercise. Even though you may not have an engineering or employee benefits background, this will still be a valuable exercise in helping you crystallise your own thoughts on your strengths and weaknesses as they apply to various jobs.

Ask yourself how many points you could score against the job specification. Apart from anything else it will give you a chance to get used to interpreting the 'newspeak' of recruitment advertisements in general.

For the moment it is important to understand what a job specification is because *we want you to write your own.* Not only will it help you search out the more obscure newspaper advertisements, it will give you practice if you decide to advertise yourself.

Many of us have acquired a great deal of experience which we wouldn't consider relevant to the job hunt, but in order to ensure you are including all your talents, don't be selective. For instance, if you're a housewife who has been out of the workforce for a few years and feels a little rusty on job skills, draw on your ability to organise (the home); deal with dissension (all families have some); budget well; maintain your cool in times of stress; whatever.

Now, using your experience, qualifications and skills, *draw up a job specification that suits your working profile.* Once you've done that, mull over it for a while. Does it seem a bit light-on? Have you included all your talents? What can you (honestly) add to make you a more impressive candidate?

Rewrite the specification until it reads like one in the newspaper. Don't be too specific. As you've probably noticed with our examples above, they are worded rather broadly to appeal to potential winners who may or may not have the specific skills the organisation is seeking. Is your specification too defined? Remember, the bigger the picture you paint, the more jobs will be in your grasp.

Once you have written down your own personal job specification you can start matching it with the situations vacant advertisements in the newspaper. After a while you'll start to see emerging careers that you hadn't considered, in areas that initially would have seemed alien.

If you're really keen, and have had some dealings with personnel consultants or executive selection firms (it would help your case if you develop a friendship with a consultant), perhaps you should send them your personal specification and ask for advice on what careers might best suit you. Ask your business contacts for advice. If you don't want to be seen as self-seeking (perhaps you don't want colleagues to know you're searching around), use the old trick of saying a friend is looking for job advancement or a new career. Could they suggest an occupation that might be suitable? Chances are you'll get some feedback.

Answering the advertisement

In most cities, Saturday is the big day for the newspaper job-hunters. All the major morning papers, plus evening and national papers, have reams of ads studding their pages, so it's likely you'll find something that gels with your personal and professional criteria. Don't forget trade magazines, local press, industry magazines, circulars, and if you're prepared to move to find the ideal job, interstate publications.

Remember you're playing a numbers game—be sure you treat this approach as a professional exercise. Sending out your résumé with a generic letter detailing your enthusiasm for the job won't guarantee success. Employers or recruit-ment agencies can receive hundreds of responses for every ad placed, and that makes for tough competition.

THERE ARE A NUMBER OF DIFFERENT FACTORS TO WATCH OUT FOR:

- *Don't limit yourself to one newspaper.* Advertisements are expensive these days—so don't assume that all ads will be in all publications. We regularly run advertisements for our clients in *The Financial Review* which are not repeated in *The Sydney Morning Herald,* for instance. The same is true for *The Australian,* which is good for specific vacancies on a national basis. Companies may choose it in preference to the local Saturday paper, even if they only want local exposure. So read the lot! And if you fancy working in another State, you should subscribe to its main daily's Saturday edition.

- *Don't be misled by headings*—different advertisements convey different meanings. Not all people who write recruitment advertisements are professional ad writers, and they are not necessarily the best communicators in the world. When you look into it, a career management opportunity might turn out to be an engineering or a marketing job. So, while it often means spending many hours each week tediously poring over newspapers, it's important to go through every advertisement and interpret it.

- *Don't hesitate to respond to ads that are a little above the position you're seeking.* There's often a chance that a ripple effect has occurred down the line and there are other job vacancies. By aiming higher, you'll be placing yourself in line for potential hidden jobs. Keep in mind that when a job is advertised, it's usually a sign of change within the company, division or department, so such an approach could work in your favour.

- 'Package' and 'dollars' mean different things to different people. An ad advertising an $80 000 package might include fringe benefits tax, superannuation, car, telephone, club memberships, travel allowances—the lot! In other cases companies *undersell* themselves. They advertise $50 000 plus benefits, and the benefits could be worth $30 000. It's another example of keeping an open mind. The job you might think beneath you at $50 000 plus benefits is actually an $80 000 job, and another job that you might think is up your street as a $60 000 package might only be $40 000 plus benefits. You can always find out what the salary and package entails in the interview and you'll find that most companies will be flexible with remuneration if they are impressed with you.

- If you are flexible on remuneration, don't mention your current salary when applying for a job. You'll be screened out by stating that you earn $25 000 or $50 000 if the job is paying $35 000. If you are asked about salary, give a broad range that might be acceptable and add 'depending on the scope and range of responsibility'. The most important thing when replying to newspaper ads is to impress with your credentials and be offered *an interview*. Salary is something that should be discussed *at* the interview and not earlier.
- If you think the ad is *nearly* a match with your credentials, always respond. Don't undersell yourself. Ads are usually placed because a general business need exists. In this case, send your résumé with a covering letter indicating your general interest and highlighting that, although your credentials are not specifically matched, your background would be valuable to the position.

Overall, don't pitch yourself too low: read the ad and look for the key points. There will always be some clues about the job on offer, the things that they are really looking for, and this will not only influence how you write your telephone script (*see* Step 6, Packaging Your Assets) but also the tone of your covering letter and possibly even your résumé. It will certainly affect the first stages of the interview. If you don't fully understand the framework of the ad, you will go into the interview with vague or false assumptions. This could irritate the interviewer, resulting in the interview getting off to a bad start.

Here are a few insider tips on the dos and don'ts of responding:

- Send your résumé and covering letter immediately—or you may find you are too late.
- Ensure your résumé is concise and attractive. State all the attributes you may have gained in your career to date that

will make the consultant/company want to call you for an interview. *(See* Step 6 Section 1, Writing an effective résumé.)

- Ensure your résumé and covering letter are addressed personally to the person handling the position. If necessary, call the company to get their name.

- Phone the contact person *first thing* Monday morning to say your résumé is in the mail and to ask for an appointment to discuss the position. Recruiters and personnel departments often start work at 8 am so don't wait until 9 am or you could be the tenth person off the rank. It's important to call while the contact is fresh—the screening procedure tightens with each good candidate. Use this call to get additional information *and* to make a good initial impression by demonstrating enthusiasm and relevance in terms of experience.

- If you are dealing with a recruitment firm, they will only put the best three or four candidates up to the client. In many cases we have turned around jobs in forty-eight hours because the first five calls presented the right people.

ADVERTISING YOURSELF

Running an advertisement to attract a possible employer is an unusual approach—but if it works, you work.

The key is to choose the right paper or the right magazine. Placing an advertisement in a major metropolitan or national newspaper to advertise your own skills may not be as useful as running it in a human resources magazine or an engineering or banking industry journal whose readers are genuinely interested in your background.

Local press would be useful too if you have got skills which could be utilised in the local community—but being industry specific is probably your best bet.

When composing your advertisement it's vital to keep some 'dos' and 'don'ts' in mind. Do be specific and keep to the key selling points of your background. Don't make it too detailed by trying to fit too much in.

MARKETING MANAGER
30 years experience to solve your problems

Exposure to fast-moving consumer package goods
and interested in joining a dynamic company
at marketing or general management level.
Sydney preferred but would move interstate
for interesting assignment.
Strengths: advertising, market research and new
product development.
Phone or Fax 9392 1622/3

When you do get the call—and you should invite your respondents to telephone rather than write because most won't take the time to reply in writing—you should be opened-minded and enthusiastic, even if the person on the other end of the phone isn't initially talking about the sort of things you think you want to hear. They have taken the time to call you, so they must have something in mind. Remember, the minute that phone call starts, you're already being evaluated.

Be prepared to elaborate on your preferences, the things you are really interested in and also the skills and attributes you think you have to offer, in more detail than you provided in the advertisement.

Initially, however, try to put yourself in the driving seat. Ask good questions—get the caller to talk about their company and the opportunity they have in mind before you have to part with too much information yourself. Then you can position your responses in a more relevant way.

Your response to the calls could go something like this:

Thank you for taking the time to call me. My advertisement was fairly general but what was it that interested you and what particular opportunity are you looking to fill? Knowing this I can respond more specifically to your needs rather than sit here and tell you over the phone that I am the greatest thing since 'sliced bread', when I may not necessarily be what you're after.

That's a polite response, putting the ball firmly in the caller's court and soliciting information before you have to respond.

USING AN INTERMEDIARY 4

The use of intermediaries—headhunters, executive search consultants, employment agencies—has rapidly increased. For very senior jobs, this is now the preferred way of locating the right employee for senior positions.

An intermediary can source and attract people and discuss various career opportunities with candidates objectively, impartially and, more importantly, confidentially.

Choosing good staff is a skill in itself and employers recognise that not everyone is good at spotting talent.

Reputable recruitment companies have experience in doing just that. It is in the recruiter's interest to place good candidates in the right jobs and win the approval—and future custom—of the client company. The recruiter needs to understand the position that is to be filled and be able to pen an appealing advertisement that will catch the reader's curiosity, whetting their appetite to apply, and then, if they are the right candidate, persuading them that it is the right move.

In order to be successful in business the recruiter must satisfy *both* parties. The client company must be pleased with the new employee, and the employee must be enthused with all the elements of the new job. And if the candidates short-listed don't come up to scratch, it's the recruiters who are held responsible.

The recruitment industry is broken into three parts. The *executive search firms* or *headhunters* handle the top echelon of non-advertised recruitment jobs (usually over $200 000) or where the company is seeking a specialist and advertising is not likely to work. Because they only work for clients, some executive search firms can be elitist, so if you write to them directly, make sure you point out your credentials and your areas of interest so they can quickly recognise the value in having you on their files.

The second section is what's commonly known as advertising recruitment or, in the industry jargon, *executive selection firms*. They are the companies which advertise in newspapers on a regular basis. The salaries offered range between $40 000 to $150 000 and occasionally up to $200 000. Many also stray into the search market, so be aware that what they advertise is only a percentage of the jobs on their books. Some firms are national and have a traditional background of soliciting résumés through advertisements. *They are client-driven as well as candidate-driven* so they tend to be more prepared to entertain direct approaches by candidates than firms which are exclusively executive search. Morgan & Banks is both a *search* and *selection* company.

The third segment of the recruitment industry is normally described as the *employment agency*. It is usually associated with non-professional and clerical staff, although a number of agencies do occasionally place graduates or people in the early stages of executive careers.

These agencies also handle *contract* and *temporary work* assignments. They can be a good starting point if you are simply looking for paid employment while you continue your career search.

A candidate pursuing an opportunity through a contract or temporary intermediary should not lose sight of the fact that *for a significant percentage of people, contract or temporary work has led to a permanent appointment.* Position yourself accordingly. Make your availability for full-time work known. Self-promote whilst on the contract assignment by creating such a good impression, adding such value, that they will want to offer you a full-time job. Certainly have your résumé dusted off and ready to roll.

Approaching a recruitment company

To precipitate an interview with a recruitment company you need a generic approach to selling yourself—a covering letter and résumé that highlights your *general* abilities.

If they are too busy to see you immediately (remember they earn fees by filling jobs, not by interviewing people) then make sure your résumé is set out in such a way that when it is registered into their database, it is easy to identify what your background is and how it might be made relevant to job opportunities.

If they can't see you right now, because they're too busy filling other jobs, at least when something relevant comes up your résumé will jump out at them!

Recognise that recruitment firms often have a number of people who specialise in different areas. It may be necessary for you to tender more than one résumé, as the retailing specialist may not necessarily hand over your résumé to the finance industry specialist, yet your skills may be applicable to both areas. An integrated database can automatically fill this gap but some firms have not made that investment yet. You could pose the question as to how your details will be retrieved when an opportunity arises in the future. A vague response should be questioned more rigorously.

Equally important: many small firms only operate in one sector or industry, so it is essential that you register what their particular specialisation is and tailor your covering letter and résumé accordingly.

Remember the old adage for selling yourself: *make it easy for the buyer to understand what you can offer them*. This means selling the benefits of what you can do for an organisation, not the features of what you think you have done.

An important point to note is that all ethical recruitment or employment agencies will tell you exactly where they are planning to send your details before they release them. If they don't, you should certainly ask them to. Not only will it prevent your résumé being 'spread around the place' but if you have a number of different irons in the fire it will ensure there is no risk of duplication.

WORKING EFFECTIVELY WITH RECRUITING FIRMS AND AGENCIES

The recruitment industry has grown steadily in recent years, no doubt helped by the trend towards outsourcing and engaging specialists for specific tasks. Furthermore, there has been a major increase in the number of 'players' in the industry through the formation of a wide variety of 'boutique' or smaller recruitment companies.

The recruitment companies therefore control a sizeable share of the job market and you need to deal effectively with them to maximise your job-search chances. Notwithstanding this we strongly suggest that you take a balanced approach to your job search and not just rely on recruiters. That is, devote plenty of time to networking, cold calling, direct mail and responding to ads placed by employers.

In dealing with recruiters and agencies, whether for permanent or contract positions, it is critical to *establish* and *maintain* the right sort of relationship. The relationship can begin either through a direct approach on your part or via a response to an advertisement.

Making the initial introduction

Early in the job-search process you should introduce yourself to the recruitment firms or agencies that are active in your chosen field. This could be two or three or as many as ten or twelve. It is a myth that you can introduce yourself to too many recruiters—none of them dominate their markets and business is usually spread among them. The secret is to control the process and insist that recruiters ask permission before doing anything with your résumé. Reciprocally, you should be open and honest with recruiters by keeping them informed of your own activities. In this way no one will trip over themselves and you will maximise your exposure to the available market.

The best method of introduction is an initial phone call. This presupposes that you have done your research and know who to ask for. Remember that recruitment consultants tend to work in specific disciplines, industries and even salary ranges. Too often time is wasted communicating with recruiters not in the best position to help. By watching the newspaper ads over a period of weeks, you will quickly pinpoint the right firms and even the contacts within those firms. If you haven't been able to isolate the exact contact, ring up and ask who looks after your portfolio.

Now you can make the call. Some tips are:

- Recruiters are busy and difficult to get on to. Keep trying. Leave a couple of messages but beyond this keep calling. Ask for appropriate times to get on to your target.
- Be direct and open. Announce who you are and that you are calling to introduce yourself because you are actively job-seeking.
- Give them a very quick overview of your background and ask if this is the sort of background they are interested in. If not, which of their consultants or other firms would be?
- Ask for the next step—'Would it be worth getting together briefly to expand on my résumé and put a face to a name?'
- If a meeting is not forthcoming, ask for commitment to receive your résumé.
- Ask what the next follow-up step from you should be, or whether should you just leave it with them. In most cases recruiters won't mind you periodically following up.

- Send your résumé immediately with a covering letter referring to this initial conversation and restating the type(s) of position(s) you are looking for.
- Remember, email is the best form of corresponding.

Hopefully your résumé will now reach the right person and be appropriately entered onto the company's database for future reference.

Responding to recruiter or agency ads

Job advertisements are the lifeblood of the recruitment industry. The ads maintain the profile of the recruiters and their companies and generate a good flow of candidates. They also create a lot of waste—answering phone calls (often hundreds), interviews, response letters, short-listing and so on. You need to be professional and efficient when responding to ads. Some tips are:

- Always respond by phone first, even if you are already known to them or on the database. The purpose of the call is to ascertain your fit and to find out about other issues you need to address in your application. You shouldn't just be wanting more detailed information, as this is wasting time and probably irritating the recruiter. Remember that you want to make a positive impression.
- You will probably be asked to send in your résumé or alternatively they will retrieve it from the database. In any case, prepare and send a very tailored application letter addressing the criteria in the ad and any further criteria you have gleaned from the phone call.
- Now just wait! Too many candidates ring to see if their information has been received or just to check on progress. These are nuisance calls as far as recruiters are concerned. On the other hand, if you haven't heard anything after about ten days, by all means follow-up.

The next important step in your relationship with recruiters may well be a face-to-face interview. This may be on a general basis to find out more about you, or more likely in response to a job and application. In either case you must be ready to perform!

The recruiter or agency interview

An initial interview with a recruiter is an extremely important meeting as it basically forms their opinion of you for life! Recruiters deal with a huge number of candidates so they will not support you if their initial opinion is not good—they will just move on. Also, there is not much you can do later to change their minds.

So to optimise your performance, here are some tips:

- Be firm about why you are looking for a job, your job preferences, career aspirations and salary expectation. Recruiters love to work with people who know what they want and are realistic about the market (particularly as far as money is concerned!). These candidates tend to perform best at their clients' interviews.
- The contemporary interview focuses very much on examples to illustrate your achievements and competencies. Have your examples well-prepared. Stick to facts, figures and specifics. Avoid generalisations.
- If the interview is in relation to a specific job, prepare your examples carefully against the selection criteria. Obviously they will be evaluating you against these.
- Be yourself, don't fake it! Recruiters will only deal with people they can get to know and trust. If they're suspicious for any reason, you're in trouble.
- If the interview covers issues not spelt out in detail in the résumé, offer to get back to the recruiter in writing immediately after the interview. It is your responsibility

to provide the recruiter with all the information they need and to make their life as easy as possible.

- At the end of the interview ask if any further information is required and what the next step should be.

It should be one of your clear responsibilities to ensure that the recruitment process flows smoothly and professionally. If you progress to interview stage with the recruiter's clients or are ultimately offered a job, here are some tips:

- If a recruiter organises a client interview for you, ask them everything you need to know to perform well. More often than not they just tell you who you are seeing, when and where. This is not enough! You need to know what the interviewer is like, who else will be there, what type of interview it will be, any issues they will be focusing on, whether you are strong or weak for the role and even what tips the recruiter has to optimise your performance. Certainly don't be a pest, but get the information a professional needs.
- Always provide the recruiter with feedback following an interview with their clients. This should not only cover how the interview went but also any concerns you have regarding the role. Restate your enthusiasm if you want the job. Remember, recruiters are trying to facilitate things at their end as well.
- Keep making life easy for the recruiter. At some stage they will want to talk to your referees. Don't just give them names and numbers but organise good times to call and ensure that your referees are prepared and expecting the call. (Do they have a copy of your latest résumé?)
- Be honest during the recruitment process. If you have other opportunities on the go let the recruiter know. You don't have to be too specific but they should be aware if other offers are coming and when. Recruiters hate

surprises. They make them look silly in front of their clients! Also, it is important if you do take a job elsewhere that you have nurtured a good relationship with the recruiters that didn't place you. You may need them in the future.

- Similarly, if you do get a job let all your recruitment-industry contacts know. They will appreciate it and may even update your file for future reference.
- Don't argue with recruiters. If they don't short-list you or consider you for a particular job they probably have good reason for doing so (even though they may not reveal it). Arguing or doubting their judgment just soils the relationship.
- Try to work with and focus on recruiters who are interested in you. If you make a particular recruiter's short-list they obviously think you're a worthy candidate. Stick with them. Don't waste time and energy on recruiters who never get back to you or never seem to have an appropriate role.

Maintaining the ultimate relationship

It is not unusual for the same recruiter (or recruitment firm) to place a candidate several times in the candidate's career. Therefore, if you are placed by a recruiter, nurture the relationship. Keep in touch every four or five months, tell them how the job is going and make sure they are on your Christmas-card list.

FOLLOWING UP
RECOMMENDATIONS

A friend has heard there's a perfect job going for you at The Giant Lollywater Corporation. So how do you follow-up? First of all you need to do a bit of research to find out the name of the person to talk to. It's always easier if you can ask for someone by name. Do a bit of networking. How did your friend find out about the job in the first place? Dead end? Okay, then ring the company direct. Ask the switchboard for the name of the section head—you must have some idea which section because presumably you have a vague idea what the job is. When you get the name, say you'll ring back. It gives you some breathing space.

Remember your networking approach: *you are not looking for a job,* you are just curious about this industry and what opportunities there are. And your assumption is that they are not necessarily interested but they might know someone who is. If they are interested they will take the bait. As we've said before, the most successful candidates always ask lots of probing questions.

It could go something like this:

Hello, Mr Jones, my name's Roger Smart. John Doe suggested I talk to you. (This can even be the person on the switchboard.)

I'm curious about the soft drinks industry. Can you recommend someone I can talk to? Someone who might be able to tell me what's going on in the way of career opportunities for young engineers. I'm prepared to consider some project work as a way of proving myself for a career in that arena.

You need to be prepared to make lots of phone calls: you will not necessarily strike 'gold' on the first call. You're an investigative journalist or a private detective and the case you are on is your own. You are pulling together a whole lot of facts and relevant information and then suddenly — breakthrough!

PACKAGING YOUR ASSETS

GETTING
THE INTERVIEW

Companies can be so swamped with applications for a job they look for reasons *not* to interview you. To avoid elimination in the first cull you need to spend time on your résumé so that it reflects the requirements of the job. In a lot of cases your 'package' will be the first contact you have with your potential employer. It has to impress and compel the person reading it to interview you.

Apart from the résumé, which of course is very important, there are other facets of the approach which will give you the edge in getting the interview. These include the accompanying covering letter and also the very important aspect of telephone technique in setting up the interview.

1WRITING AN EFFECTIVE RÉSUMÉ

In this section we will cover the basic content and detail necessary for an effective résumé, but there is *one important attribute of a successful résumé* which we would like to stress: it should be a document which explains to the reader *what it is you can do for them*—that is, the benefits you will bring to their organisation

Most people describe what they see as their achievements or their skills in a way which really sets out features rather than benefits. They fail to translate their past experience or training in a way that is easy for a potential employer to recognise as setting them apart from other applicants.

For example, a feature statement might go something like this: 'In a call centre environment responsible for assisting customers with enquiries and logging details into a computerised system.' In a contemporary résumé a benefit statement would be: 'In a call centre environment achieved top ratings for attitude, clear communications, problem solving and service levels over four consecutive customer-satisfaction surveys in the last year.'

Describing and dividing what you have actually done into easily identifiable categories of skills, knowledge and attributes assists a potential employer to assess your value to an organisation.

Remember that your résumé (or CV—there's no difference) *is not meant to get you a job, it is meant to get you an interview.*

Résumé preparation

WHAT IS A RÉSUMÉ? It is:

- a selling document;
- a source of information;
- a script for talking about yourself.

WHAT IS THE PURPOSE OF A RÉSUMÉ? Its purpose is:

- to get an interview;
- to remind someone of who you are after your meeting.

HOW MANY PARTS DOES IT HAVE AND IN WHAT ORDER SHOULD IT BE PRESENTED? It should have:

- personal details, including relevant education;
- career overview—a summary of your work experience;
- career details—a detailed record of your work experience.

Some general guidelines

There are many facts and fallacies about writing a good résumé, and depending where you turn you'll get different advice. However, by following these general guidelines you will produce a document which successfully 'sells' you.

- If you send a résumé before seeing someone, its purpose is to act as a personal selling document—one that will get you invited to an interview or for a meeting.
- A résumé is not always the first step in the process to hire someone—it may be your door-opener but you may also use it as a follow-up tool after seeing someone.
- People who receive résumés often use them for screening you 'out' rather than 'in'. Be aware that the first person to look at your résumé for a specific job may not be the person who will do the interviewing; the person culling résumés may have a list of criteria to match. Your résumé will have to at least match the criteria to ensure you are considered for an interview.

- When you get to the interview, your résumé can act as the agenda for your discussion, giving the interviewer a basis from which to find out more about you and your suitability for the job. Yes, it is acceptable to take a copy of your résumé to an interview and to refer to it as and when you need to.

- Layout and design should be legible, consistent and easy to follow, with good clear headings, a large easy-to-read font—such as Times Roman—and no typographical or grammatical errors. If the résumé is in hard copy use good quality, plain paper. (Coloured paper or a fancy border doesn't add anything unless the position in question requires a demonstration of that sort of creativity—for example, the creative area of an advertising department.)

- Do not send poor-quality photocopies. It doesn't cost much for good-quality reproductions—and this is your career we're talking about!

- Ensure pages are numbered and that your name is on each page.

- Orient your résumé towards specific (and quantifiable) achievements rather than duties and responsibilities. It should tell prospective employers everything that might interest them and nothing that will waste their time.

- Keep it honest. Don't exaggerate your experience to make your résumé sound more impressive. If it can't stand up to scrutiny in the interview you will blow your chances of getting the job.

- Write in clear, concise terms, using active words (eg. accomplished, created, enhanced, launched, negotiated, etc.) and keeping pronouns (I, we, they) to a minimum or avoid them altogether.

- Keep it succinct. Highlight particular personal achieve- ments. For example: 'During my period as manager, turnover increased 120 per cent which was acknowledged by winning an annual company award for high achievement.' If your professional experience is limited it might be wise to include memberships of clubs or organisations that show commitment to being involved.

- Do not write a novel. We suggest you keep your résumé to approximately two to four pages. It should concisely paint a picture of you and your job experience. Key points should be highlighted to develop interest and enthusiasm. Include the kind of information you would like to know if you were hiring someone. *The reviewer must be drawn to wanting to meet you in person.*

- Leave out all details of past salaries, bonus payments, superannuation contributions. This will be covered in the interview stages. Without knowing all the details of the company and the job, you might inadvertently send a message about your suitability for a particular role.

- Put your work experience and educational details in reverse chronological order, that is, *starting with the most recent.* It's easier to follow.

- Don't use a narrative style. Highlight your accomplishments in a bullet point format, then you don't need as many complete sentences—that's how you get it into two to four pages! *But be warned:* Brief points must be carefully thought out. At the interview stage your statements must be backed up by evidence—based on your track record or education.

- Be specific in your résumé. Where possible use numbers or percentages to illustrate your successes or the impact you can have. Avoid claiming complete responsibility for achievements, implying no one else deserves any credit, which is usually not the case.

- Avoid initials and jargon. Write in plain English so you're understood. There's a general consensus by good interviewers that people who *really* know their subject write and speak clearly and don't try and complicate issues.

Remember, you are supposed to be an expert on yourself. If you can't get your act together to demonstrate that you know who you are, what you have done, and what you can do in your next job, then don't expect a potential employer or a recruiter to take the same amount of interest in you as in a candidate who can articulate their potential value to an organisation.

Never send your résumé without a covering letter, fax or email.

The first page of your résumé should include your personal details—including education—and your career overview. The other pages should cover your work experience in detail.

Personal details

Personal details can be fairly brief:

- your name;
- postal address;
- telephone contact numbers—home, mobile and business, (if confidentiality is a problem at your business number, make sure you note this on your résumé);
- email and fax details.

Education

Key elements are:

- the level of education you obtained and your qualifications;
- the name of the institution;
- the years you attended various institutions.

It is vital that details of the degrees, diplomas or certificates are not misleading. Academic qualifications should not be fudged—*never claim a qualification you don't have.*

IN THE SAME SECTION YOU *CAN* INCLUDE THE FOLLOWING DETAILS:

- professional memberships—gives credibility, shows extra-curricular and intellectual interests;
- permanent residency: if you're not an Australian citizen, employers need to know that you are legally able to work in Australia and for how long;
- other languages (if fluent);
- interests and/or leisure activities (gives an insight into how you spend your time outside work). Irrelevant, you say? It could help you break the ice in the first interview if the employer has similar interests. What have you got to lose?

Career overview

This section should give a brief synopsis of your work experience. How you do this will depend on what aspects of your background you want to promote or sell to a new employer. Two possible approaches are these:

- List the companies you have worked for, the positions you have held and corresponding dates of employment. You should start with your most recent job and work backwards covering the last five to ten years of your work experience. By providing this information the reader can quickly determine your career moves and development, your industry background as well as the profile of the companies for which you have worked.
- Another approach is to state your role title and particular areas of expertise or competence. This might be followed

by a series of career highlights, grouped according to key competency areas.

Career details

Your career details should record your employment history. Start with your present job or, if you are not currently working, your previous job.

First state the dates of your employment and describe your current/previous organisation. Joe Bloggs Timber is not enough. If it produces and manufactures roof trusses, say so. Include the following information on the organisation, division, department or branch:

- approximate turnover or budget in dollars—to indicate size;
- number of employees;
- main activities in terms of products or services and areas of operation.

It's important to give a feel for the size and activities of the organisation because in the absence of that information the person reviewing your résumé may assume it's a rather more simple operation than it is.

Secondly, give details of your employment which may include:

- your title;
- who you report(ed) to;
- who reports to you;
- the purpose of your job—where does it fit into the organisation?
- how big your job is—dimensions—statewide or national;
- how much accountability and/or responsibility you have for budgets/staff;
- the key duties and responsibilities of your position;

- how good are you—did you 'add value' to the job? Did you effect any special achievements?

Continue in reverse chronological order to detail your work experience. Remember you only have one to three pages in which to provide these career details, so information on earlier roles can be kept to a minimum.

Note: Recruiters and employers are looking for achievements. They don't want a list of job descriptions, they want to know what your activities were and what you achieved while working for the organisation.

Following is a sample of a well-constructed résumé.

JEFF WILLIAMS

50 Sydney Place

Sydney NSW 2000

222 2222 Home Phone & Fax

0419 444444 Mobile & Messages

jwilliams@internet.com.au

FORMAL QUALIFICATIONS

M.B.A.—Macquarie University

B.E.—University of New South Wales

PROFESSIONAL AFFILIATIONS

Fellow, Institution of Engineers, Australia

Fellow, Australian Institute of Management

Board Member, Australian Chamber of Manufactures

CAREER OVERVIEW

Enterprise Engineering Limited	**Feb 89–Jun 99**
General Manager—Australia	May 95–Jun 99
General Manager—S.E. Asia	Jan 92–Apr 95
Sales Director—Australia	Feb 89–Dec 92

Repetition Manufacturing Limited	Feb 85–Jan 89
Sales Manager—Australia	Jan 87–Jan 89
Sales Manager—NSW	Feb 85–Dec 86
Rolled Products Limited	**Jan 75–Jan 85**
Sales Executive—NSW	Jul 81–Jan 85
Engineering Manager	Jan 77–Jun 81

CAREER IN DETAIL

ENTERPRISE ENGINEERING LIMITED   *Feb 89–Jun 99*

A diversified heavy engineering and manufacturing group operating in the Asia-Pacific region with total sales of $350 million and 850 employees. Manufacturing facilities in Sydney, Melbourne, Djakarta and Manila.

General Manager Australia   May 95–Jun 99

Profit centre responsibility for the Australian business with a turnover of $250 million and 500 employees.

Achievements

- Successful rationalisation of the business through closure of manufacturing sites in Sydney and Melbourne— redundancy of 75 employees.

- Negotiated a company-wide enterprise agreement which resulted in productivity improvements of 5% and 8% in the last two years.

- Increased profit in 98/99 to $35.6m, up 19% on previous year.

- Successful acquisition of a competitor in key markets, for a cost of $37m.

- Penetrated new markets (via product development), contributing $39m to the bottom line.

General Manager—S.E. Asia   Jan 92–Apr 95

This was a start-up role in the region, with the mandate of penetrating the large South-East Asian automotive market.

Achievements

- Researched, negotiated and finalised the necessary joint venture partnership.

- Established branch sales offices in Djakarta, Manila, Bangkok and Shanghai.

- Project managed the construction of the first and major manufacturing facility in the region—project cost $65m, brought in on time and 5% under budget.

- Through successful negotiation of four long-term contracts grew revenue from zero to $87m p.a. in just three years.

- Achieved preferred supplier status with Mazda and Nissan through quality assurance initiatives.

Sales Director—Australia   Feb 89–Dec 92

Sales responsibility for Australia, with a revenue of $150m, offices in all capital cities, and total sales force of 55.

Achievements

- Restructured the sales force to be product focused rather than regionally focused—headcount reduction of 15 and improved customer service.

- Renegotiated three major contracts with a value of $57m, resulting in a 10% lift in profitability.

- Successfully launched a new product line in June 1989, ultimately contributing $25m to revenue in the 91/92 financial year.

- Developed the strategic plan for the expansion of the business into S.E. Asia (and subsequently spearheaded the project).

REPETITION MANUFACTURING LIMITED   Feb 85–Jan 89

This company manufactured components for the automotive industry, with a revenue of $125m and sales offices in Sydney, Melbourne, Brisbane and Adelaide.

Sales Manager—Australia   Jan 87–Jan 89

Managed a sales force of 25 across four states.

Achievements

- Successfully sought and negotiated two new contracts increasing company revenue by 23% in the 88/89 financial year.

- Developed and established six new product lines, thus 'closing the door' on a major competitor.

- Introduced a sales incentive scheme, lifting sales force productivity by 30%.

Sales Manager—NSW   **Feb 85–Dec 86**

Managed 15 sales staff with a State target of $80m p.a.

Achievements

- Redefined sales regions and accountabilities, resulting in the redundancy of five sales engineers.

- Consequently increased customer service, with an increase in revenue of 15% in the 85/86 financial year.

- Secured a major new customer ($8.5m p.a.) through a strategic alliance agreement.

The covering letter, fax or email

As part of the strategy for getting the interview, it's important to have an effective covering note to accompany your résumé. It may be influential in deciding whether or not you get the interview.

An advertisement placed in the paper or on the Internet might elicit 150 responses. *People are not looking for reasons to interview, they are looking for reasons to reject so that a manageable list of possible candidates can be drawn up.*

The aim of the covering note is to get the interview selector to read your résumé. You need to show why your background is relevant to the position. You need to stress your interest in the role and how you fit the selection criteria.

Under no circumstances send a standard letter or note. If you have to compose 100 covering letters for 100 jobs then each should be carefully tailored. This is the one real opportunity you have, prior to the interview, to really pitch for the position and to present your sincere and genuine interest.

Unless it is stipulated in the advertisement, it is not necessary to hand write a covering letter.

If you are responding to an advertised position through a recruitment company you'll usually be given a contact name, but often organisations advertising positions themselves request that you send your résumé to The Human Resources

Manager. In the first case it's easy to personalise your covering note. In the second it's not. Don't fall into the trap of addressing the note to 'Dear Sir'—for a start, the HR Manager is just as likely to be a woman. In such an instance you can choose to dispense with a salutation or you can phone the organisation to find out the name of the person to whom your application should be sent.

The covering note or letter (see example on next page) must include the details of the position you are applying for, and where and when the job was advertised. If applicable, also include the reference number of the job, and reference to any telephone conversation you may have had with them in relation to the position.

THE COVERING NOTE SHOULD:

- highlight specific aspects of your background that relate to the position or company in question. *Don't rely on the reader to interpret why you fit the position.* Be specific: 'You will notice my background involves five years of marketing in consumer package goods which relates specifically to the advertised requirements of your client.'
- talk about your motivation. Why are you responding to the position? Is it the company or the job? Do a sales pitch on yourself because if your letter or note doesn't read persuasively, you are not likely to get the interview.
- do not repeat verbatim the information in your résumé—it will make the letter too long and may frustrate the reviewer. Once again, the best approach is to focus on those experiences or competencies outlined in the advertisement.
- end with a proactive statement. For example, 'I look forward to meeting you at an interview to further discuss my fit with the role'; 'As agreed, I look forward to obtaining a date and time for an interview'; 'Finally, I confirm our appointment for Tuesday the 24th at 10 am'.

The following is an example of a covering letter or note.

Terence Davis
17 Haywood Avenue
ROSEBAY NSW 2029
(02) 9911 1111

18 January 1999

Ms Deborah Blaze
Recruitment Consultant
Morgan & Banks Limited
Level 11, Grosvenor Place
225 George Street
SYDNEY NSW 2000

Dear Deborah

RE: FINANCIAL ACCOUNTANT—REFERENCE NO.
AIF/3002 THE SYDNEY MORNING HERALD,
16 JANUARY 1999

As mentioned in our telephone conversation today, I was very attracted by your advertisement and believe my background is an excellent match with your client's requirement.

You will see from my résumé that I have developed a wide range of technical skills while employed with Price Waterhouse and then MLC. In particular, the following are relevant:

- Qualified chartered accountant with three years audit experience.
- Extensive knowledge of statutory reporting requirements gained in audit project teams and latterly as part of a small finance group.
- Excel and Word for Windows skills used daily in reporting activities.

- Given sole responsibility for managing implementation of new procedure relating to fringe benefits tax administration. Implementation was successful and completed on time.

I look forward to meeting with you at an interview and will call in the week commencing 22 January to arrange a mutually convenient time.

Yours sincerely
TERENCE DAVIS

A word of warning

While you should present yourself as confident and in control, avoid being flippant or disrespectful. When you don't personally know the recruiter or interviewer, it's safer to err on the side of caution and professionalism. The covering letter is part of the interview-getting process—if you come across as cocky, the interview selector will strike you from the list before you have a chance to really show what you are made of! However, you can be creative without being cocky!

Referees and references—a case of give and take

Providing references and the names of referees to prospective employers is a case of give and take: it may surprise you to realise that while some references or referees will be given by you, some they will obtain themselves. They might just happen to know someone who was a colleague of yours when you worked for Jones, Jones & Jones, and in the course of a general conversation they may solicit an opinion about you without necessarily revealing why. This sort of informal reference checking goes on all the time.

Choosing a referee

There are some guidelines you should follow:

- It is likely you will be asked to provide at least two referees and that these people will be contacted by telephone for their comments.
- Always ask permission to use a person as a referee and be sure to explain the nature of the position and the essential and desirable skills for the position, as this is what the referee will be asked to comment on.
- Referees should certainly be people who have knowledge of your academic, professional or working life.
- Where possible choose those people who are able to articulate their views succinctly and those who are seen in the eyes of the potential employer as being credible. In most instances people who have recently managed you should be on your list of referees. In other words, you want as much clout as possible.

The referees you select may vary with different jobs. If the role in question relates to skills you haven't used for ten years then you might have to search out some older contacts, more relevant to this particular job. In a different situation, you may use more recent referees, such as people related to your last job or your last educational qualification.

Talk to your main referees *before* you begin the job-search process. Not only will you find out what it is they will say about you when it comes to the crunch, but it may help shape how you approach your job search. Ideally they should be people whom you rely on to give an opinion about what it is you are good at and the environments in which you will be most motivated to achieve. On the other hand, if there are issues on which you disagree, for example a difficult working relationship with another team member, it is important to know how your referee will handle this information during a reference check. There are times when you may need to be honest and objective in flagging a possible negative to a prospective employer—nobody likes surprises late in the recruitment process.

Don't submit the names and contact details of your referees until you get to the interview stage unless you have exceptional written references and you want to attach them to your résumé. It is unusual for prospective employers to check your references out before they have met you.

Employers can't really ask the detailed questions they should put to a referee until they identify your strengths and weaknesses during the interview process.

If you have been out of the workforce for some time, your references will be commenting more on your character. Rather than a quantifiable track record that is easily measurable, you will be asking your referees to validate that you have *potential* to do the task in question.

Don't underestimate and forget references that relate to your personal life. If you have been an active, outgoing student, or as a mother and housewife you have accomplished certain tasks in relation to your child's school, include these achievements. In your situation, a potential employer is focusing far more on what you can do in the future, rather than what you have done in the past. Anything that reinforces the fact that you are an achiever, that you are organised, and that you have the respect and the support of other people, will work to your advantage.

SETTING UP THE INTERVIEW— TELEPHONE TECHNIQUE

The telephone plays an integral part in getting a job. Your telephone technique needs to be perfected. You cannot rely on your résumé or the interview to clinch the deal.

If you are making the call, remember *the object of the exercise is to move to the next phase*, either to solicit further information on the organisation, gain an interview, follow one up or, better still, follow-up on a job offer.

PREPARATION IS THE KEY:

- Before you dial the number, make sure you know exactly who are you going to ask for, what your call is in connection with, and what you want to achieve.
- Think through what it is you are going to say and how you are going to say it, keeping it brief and to the point.
- If necessary, have some basic points written out on a pad in front of you so that you can move logically and swiftly through the phone call. This will give the impression of an organised person who means business, as opposed to someone who is thinking out loud.
- Always have a pen and paper ready to take notes for later inclusion in your workbook.
- Never eat, smoke or chew gum when you are on the phone.
- Don't waffle—people just don't have the time and they will assume you're *always* tentative in your approach.
- Once you achieve your objective, keep quiet and close the conversation.

- If you are phoning a consultant unsolicited and unrelated to an advertised position, *don't* call on Monday morning. They will be sorting out the advertised jobs and won't want to be distracted.
- Never leave a message unless it's necessary or routine. Then *you* are in control—when you ring back you're calling the shots. And when you do get through you are confident your message is going to the right person.
- Don't try to be too clever and bypass support staff— it's their job to screen calls. Sometimes you can use them to your advantage by getting them on side and asking them for help.
- Make sure your household is tuned in to the fact that you are involved in the serious business of getting a job and the need to take your calls or messages in such a way that you don't miss any opportunities.

There is no fixed formula or script here, but the best possible result comes when you are prepared.

Once you've galvanised yourself into serious networking, you must always be prepared for an *on-the-spot telephone interview*.

- A potential employer may call you in response to your résumé or an enquiry you have made;
- You might get a follow-up call to an interview which has already taken place;
- In some situations a company may decide to screen a number of candidates over the phone;
- You may be networking and someone decides to interview you on the spot.

If a call catches you off-guard, don't panic.

Thank you for calling, Mr Jones. Would you mind waiting a moment, I'll just take the call in my office/study/workroom/ studio.

Head immediately for the area you have set aside for work and where you have access to your workbook (remember our recommendation to have an organised workbook), your résumé, and a pad and pencil. Take a deep breath, relax—you are now in control!

With your workbook handy you can quickly refer to the name of the person calling, the organisation, or some other reference. It should be well set out so you can trace your last phone call to that organisation, when you wrote to them, what you said, and background information on the organisation itself. You will sound focused and organised and you can confidently launch into a couple of prepared questions (from your research and notes) about the job and what it entails. Let's face it, it doesn't sound good if a prospective employer calls you and they have to remind you what it is you applied for three weeks ago, or the details of an advertisement.

Writing a telephone script that impresses

You must be prepared and be able to communicate within 20 or 30 seconds:

- who you are;
- what your phone call is about;
- then get across your message precisely and persuasively.

The examples provided can be used as a guide, but, of course, your call has to be tailored not only to you and your background, but also to the organisation, the person and the role.

WITH THE TELEPHONE SCRIPT THERE ARE THREE GOLDEN RULES:

- make sure you have a relaxed voice;
- make sure you are not distracted during the phone call;
- and above all, don't speak in a rushed or unfriendly manner.

Why not phone a few of your friends and ask if you can practise your telephone script on them? Then get their appraisal on your level of confidence and relaxation.

Example 1

You have made a decision you want to work for this company and you are taking a direct approach:

You Mr Jones?
Contact Yes?
You My name is Roger Smart. Is it convenient to speak?
Contact Yes, what's it about?
You Mr Jones, I have been an operations manager in the food industry with over ten years experience in organising manufacturing and distribution activities in a successful and profitable business. I am looking for opportunities with other market leaders and wondered if you can help.
Contact Well, yes, but I wonder how. We're not actually looking for anyone at the moment.
You I understand but hoped to set up a short meeting with you to discuss your leading position in the industry and a couple of distribution initiatives I was responsible for last year and which led to increased revenue in the first quarter. Would you have half an hour to spare next week some time? How would Thursday at 10 am suit you?

Example 2

Here you are merely exploring your options:

You Hello, Mr Jones?
Contact Yes?
You My name is Elizabeth Smith and I wondered whether you have a moment to speak ... (pause)
Contact Yes, what's it about?

You You may recall that I wrote to you on 15 January in relation to the prospect of employment with your organisation. I was wondering whether you had half an hour so that I could perhaps enlarge on the information contained in that résumé, and my genuine interest in joining your company.

This should lead to a friendly exchange at least, and hopefully to a commitment to interview at a particular time, date and place.

SELLING YOUR ASSETS

THE INTERVIEW

The short time you spend at a job interview could have a dramatic effect on YOUR short and long-term career prospects. It is therefore important that you perform well, because no matter how good your career record is to date, the employment interview remains an important step towards fulfilment of your ambitions.

This is your opportunity to demonstrate your personal attributes, your strengths, personality, your ability to communicate and how you react under pressure.

Listed below are some general tips.

Develop rapport

To ensure effective communication, it is very important to develop a good rapport with the person interviewing you. Of course, this is sometimes difficult, particularly if you 'really

159

want the job'. However, you must relax—get that high-pitched or tense tone out of your voice—and appear to be calm and self-assured at all times.

One of the most simple ways of helping this is to *smile* a lot. Yes, when appropriate, smile. Not a grin but a genuine, warm smile.

Ask yourself seriously: do you smile during the course of conversation?

Try this as an experiment. Stand in front of your mirror and role-play both the interviewer and yourself. Ask questions, make statements, then answer them. Let yourself disagree with the imaginary interviewer. With a straight face say: 'While I accept your point of view, with respect, I disagree because my experience has shown that you just can't manage people that way.'

Now repeat exactly the same statement but with a slight, intelligent smile on your face. The impact on the listener is enormous.

Relax the interviewer!?

If you put the interviewer at ease they will immediately feel more comfortable with you, which will work to your benefit. Don't assume you're the only one who's tense. A lot of people doing the hiring are also a little tense when they conduct interviews.

Here's a hint. To start the conversation rolling, choose a subject that is not directly related to your being there. You may have noticed something on your way into the company's offices—noticeboards, magazines, or articles in reception, or perhaps something on the interviewer's wall. You will come across as a warm, pleasant and *likeable* person, rather than only a highly intelligent and impressive individual who was a little cool (even though this may have been because you were nervous). Whether you get the job or not can often come down to the basics (interviewers will often make up their mind on gut feeling): Do I like you? Do I think you are going to fit into my organisation? Do I trust you? Would I buy from you? Would my customers take advice from you?

Ask good questions

This is a *big tip!* Don't just tell the interviewer how wonderful you are and how good your achievements have been. Demonstrate you have done your homework, that you are really listening and you understand what's going on. You can do this by *asking relevant questions* about the company and the job in question. Taking an interest in the big picture, that is, the company, as well as the job itself, will have a positive influence on the interviewer. If, in the limited time of the interview, you can ask one or two questions that actually make that interviewer think about the answer, or better still, maybe cover issues they hadn't even thought of, then you really are on the home stretch.

You can take a very direct approach when doing this. Here's a question which can be used when applying for most positions. Rarely used by candidates, it can make a lasting impression with interviewers, particularly if they have seen three or four other candidates for the same job that day.

It covers management style, and at a very personal level asks the interviewer or prospective boss exactly *what it is they are looking for in the new employee and how they are going to measure their performance.*

The question might go something like this:

Mr Jones, I understand the position in question and I now have a good feel for the department and the division. But at a personal level, if I am successful in getting this job, what would you expect of me in terms of daily activity and performance, and what do you see as the critical factors in achieving the best possible results, thereby ensuring my success?

In effect, what you're asking is *how are you going to manage me* and *how will you get the best out of me*. And by getting the interviewer to 'come clean', a much more healthy level of dialogue is going to take place.

The ultimate objective is to develop the sort of rapport you'd like to think you'll have with this prospective employer a week after you've started the job. In other words, you'll no longer be selling and trying to impress but listening and getting down to basics. This will produce a more effective result and ensure there are no misunderstandings (for example, where the job looks right but is wrong—*see* Step 2, Stocktaking Your Assets).

Demonstrate enthusiasm

An employer is often willing to give someone a chance, even if they don't have all the right skills, *because they are enthusiastic and passionate about a particular job*. Demonstrate how keen you are. Do your homework and be definite: I want this job. Then follow up tenaciously. It does work!

1 THE TRADITIONAL INTERVIEW

Now, let's clarify one important part of any job. All organisations, from volunteer groups to major corporations, need employees who can use their skills and experience to diagnose and solve problems. Whenever people are hired, it's most important that they become part of the solution, not add to the problem. Identifying weaknesses in the organisation is relatively easy—it's solving them that takes talent, so don't be too quick to judge.

So what's the magic answer to proving your ability as a problem-solver? It comes back to how well you carried out your job search. To the interviewer, if you've done a thorough, confident and professional job hunt it's likely you'll conduct your job in the same manner.

The only way to approach your potential employer is by having done your research.

Preparation will make or break the interview

Preparation is the first essential step towards a successful interview. Company interviewers are continually amazed at the number of applicants who drift into their offices without any apparent preparation and only the vaguest idea of what they are going to say.

It's important to clarify the following before the interview:

- Know the exact place and time of the interview; the interviewer's full name; the correct pronunciation; and their title.
- Find out specific facts about the company—where its plants, stores or offices are located; what its products and services are; what its growth has been; what its growth potential is. There are a number of research publications providing this kind of information. *(See* Step 4 Section 6, How to Get Information.) But just to recap, among the most helpful are:

The Business Who's Who of Australia;
Kompass Australia;
Jobson's Year Book of Public Companies;
The Stock Exchange Research Handbook;
Web sites.

All are available in a public library. A brokerage office or your bank may also be able to supply you with pertinent information.

Note: Don't make pronouncements about the company's philosophy—that's dangerous. Just have some basic facts at your disposal. You're an expert on yourself, not them. (Not yet, anyway!)

- Visualise issues the company could be facing and how they relate to the job.
- Visualise the situation/ways you could possibly work there.
- Consider what you want from the job and what you can offer in return.
- Know who *you* are *(see* Step 2 Section 1, Knowing Yourself).
- Refresh your memory on the facts and figures of your *present/former* employer. You will be expected to know a lot about the company.
- Prepare the questions you will ask during the interview. (*See* the checklist of some questions you can and should ask on page 168.)
- For men and women, dress in a dark (blue or grey if possible) business suit. Do not wear sports clothes. Pay attention to all facets of your dress and grooming: men—don't forget to put a belt through the trouser loops; women—day-wear with a business flavour, not an 'evening' look or anything too flashy.

Be prepared to answer questions

STANDARD INTERVIEW QUESTIONS INCLUDE:

- Why did you choose this particular vocation? What do you really want to do in life?
- What do you want to be doing in your career five years from now? Ten years from now?
- What was the size of your last salary review? When was it?

- What style of management gets the best from you? Who was your best boss? Why?
- What interests you about our products or services?
- Can you get recommendations from previous employers?
- What have you learnt from some of the jobs you have held? Which did you enjoy the most?
- What have you done that shows initiative in your career?
- What are your strongest skills?
- How do your skills relate to the company's needs?
- How can you contribute to the company?
- What are you looking for in your next job?
- What do you know about us?
- What do you think determines a person's progress in a good company?
- How do you spend your spare time? What are your hobbies?
- What does teamwork mean to you?
- Have you saved any money?
- What's the best book you've read recently?

Some questions fall into the 'open probe' category, and if you are not ready for them, any one of them can weaken your presentation and be a confidence-sapper, so be ready.

Open probe questions are difficult because they strike right at the heart of issues and require more than a yes/no answer.

- *Why did you leave your last job? Why do you want to change jobs?*
  Have a positive answer—talk about what worked in your last jog, as well as what hasn't. Confident, coherent and logical explanations are critical to the interview process.

- *What is your greatest strength/weakness?*
  Have some answers ready—even weaknesses can be
  presented positively, especially if you are doing something
  about them.
- *Tell me about yourself?* This is a chance to show your
  communication skills—don't ramble, and stick to
  business-related aspects of yourself where possible.
- *What sort of income are you looking for?*
  Always give a range if the interviewer pushes for an
  amount, but try to be general.
- *Are you willing to travel/relocate?*
  Don't be too exact on the amount of travelling time—
  appear flexible. If you are willing to relocate, be specific
  about how open-minded you are.
- *Why should I hire you?*
  Here's a chance to review your strengths and show how
  you can make a big contribution. Sell your *benefits,* not
  your *features. (See* Step 6, Packaging Your Assets.)
- *Why do you want to work for our organisation?*
  Here is a chance to show how well you did your research
  before the interview.
- *How do you react to criticism?*
  Give an example of how you accepted and benefited from
  criticism, as this can show a positive attitude to learning.
- *What did you like about your last position?*
  This gives you a chance to show that a negative situation
  does not apply to the position you are after in this company.

You probably just skimmed over these lists so we want you
to go back and read them again—carefully this time. Now
take out some paper and start writing your answers—
truthful answers that demonstrate your achievements. You
will be put on the spot if you are not prepared.

Seemingly irrelevant questions such as *What's the best
book you've read recently?* have very little to do with the job

but it has a great deal to do with the type of person you are. The interviewer is simply trying to assess what sort of person you are. If the answer is that you don't read, okay, but tell them what else you do when you're relaxing. It's all designed to open you up as a person.

Take *How do you spend your spare time and what are your hobbies?* Your answer can indicate whether you prefer solo activities or those more team-oriented, if you're into physical and competitive activities or whether you're more interested in intellectual pursuits. It also demonstrates how good you are at expressing yourself about an activity in which you have an interest. It gives the interviewer an idea of whether your interests will complement or conflict with your work. For instance you might be needed to attend weekend conferences but you're involved in a team activity that involves playing competitively every weekend. Or you might be a keen triathlete whose interest in swimming, running and cycling complements your career aspirations.

Let's look at another question: *What have you learned from some of the jobs you have held and which job did you enjoy the most?* The interviewer isn't looking for a description of your work history. The interviewer is searching for your real feelings about your previous employment: what—in your view—was the most important aspect of working with the company; what motivated you to search for new levels of excellence; what are you leaving with in terms of real knowledge and an understanding of the industry. The interviewer is looking for your general views, preferences and attitudes in order to assess whether you are a motivated worker or passive in your approach to a career.

What have you done that shows initiative in your career? Here the interviewer is looking for your motivations, your ability to crystallise your strengths and your ability to describe what could sometimes be intangible experiences or activities.

What do you want to be doing in your career over the next five or ten years? The interviewer is searching for your aspirations. Perhaps you have set your mind on achieving the general manager's position. Perhaps your views are so set you come across as inflexible. In some cases your aspirations may be unrealistic, or too modest, too high or low in relation to your abilities. Many candidates find this the most difficult question because they are so unsure about their own ambition and future. *This is an important question* because the employer doesn't want someone with great ambitions in a limited job that has no career stream—such a person will become frustrated and leave the organisation. Similarly, there's little point in employing a person who is happy to be a subordinate when the company is searching for a successor to the team manager.

Be prepared to ask questions

Remember that an interview is a two-way street. Through questioning, the employer will try to determine if you have the qualifications necessary to do the job. *You* must determine, through questioning, whether the company will give you the opportunity for the growth and development you seek.

HERE ARE SOME PROBING QUESTIONS YOU CAN AND *SHOULD* ASK:

- Why is this position open?
- What are the key requirements for the position?
- How is the performance measured? (Goals should be clearly defined so measurements have some objectivity.)
- How tough is your company's competition? (You should know from your research who their competitors are.)
- Are there opportunities that are unique to this job within the organisation?
- Do internal promotions meet your growth demands for management?

- What are the company's plans for the future?
- What would a successful person expect to be earning in their fourth or fifth year?
- What sort of induction and training do you normally provide?
- Do you feel I fit the key requirements of the job? From your perspective, in which areas are there gaps?
- Is there anything else you want to know about me?

Remember, many companies are hoping to employ a career person, not just a worker. Usually only three or four candidates are short-listed for a position, so presumably if you're on the short-list you will have the necessary skills and experience to carry out the job. And you must assume that your opponents for the position are equally, if not better, qualified. *So this interview will make or break you as the person the company would like to have around.* The client wants to know your motivations, your ideals and ambitions, and an element of the private you. The candidates might have very little between them, but *only one can win the job.* If you want to work with this company you must give it your best shot. And you'll only achieve this by preparation.

Ask yourself this key question: *Do I really know enough about the job, the company and how I can contribute, to make sense at the interview?*

During the course of an interview, the employer will be evaluating your *negative factors* as well as your *positive attributes.* There are some common negative factors that employers tell us they watch for in interviews. If you want to avoid rejection, your interviewer will most likely be unimpressed with:

- poor personal appearance, lack of poise;
- overbearing, overaggressive, conceited 'superiority complex', 'know-it-all' attitudes;

- inability to express thoughts clearly—poor diction or grammar;
- lack of planning for a career—no purpose or goals;
- lack of enthusiasm—passive and indifferent;
- lack of confidence—nervousness;
- over-emphasis on money—interested only in remuneration;
- evasive responses—makes excuses for unfavourable factors in record;
- lack of tact/maturity/courtesy;
- condemnation of past employers;
- failure to look the interviewer in the eye;
- limp handshake;
- lack of appreciation of the value of experience;
- failure to ask questions about the job;
- lack of preparation for interview—failure to get information about the company, resulting in inability to ask intelligent questions;
- persistent attitude of 'What can you do for me?'.

The do's and don'ts of interviews

You are being interviewed because the company wants to hire someone—not because they want to trip you up or embarrass you. Through the interaction that will take place during the interview, the interviewer will be searching out your strong and weak points, evaluating you on your qualifications, skills and intellectual qualities, and will probably probe deeply to determine your attitudes, aptitudes, stability, motivation and maturity.

- DO plan to arrive on time or a few minutes early. Late arrival for a job interview is *never* excusable.
- If presented with an application, DO fill it out neatly and completely. If you have a personal résumé, be sure the

person you release it to is the person who will actually do the hiring.

- DO greet the interviewer by their surname. If you are not sure of the pronunciation ask them to repeat it.
- DO shake hands firmly.
- DO wait until you are offered a chair before sitting. Sit upright in your chair, look alert and interested at all times. Be a good listener as well as a good talker. *Smile*.
- DO look a prospective employer in the eye while you talk with them.
- DO follow the interviewer's leads but try to get the interviewer to describe the position and the duties to you early in the interview so that you can relate your background and skills to the position.
- DO make sure that your good points get across in a factual, sincere manner. Keep in mind that you alone can sell yourself to the interviewer. You must convince the interviewer of the need for you in the organisation.
- DO always conduct yourself as if you are determined to get the job you are discussing. Never close the door on opportunity. It is better to be in the position where you can choose from a number of jobs—rather than only one.
- DO take a pen, paper and a diary with you. Then you can book the next appointment or ask for a date to follow-up the result. It looks organised!
- DON'T smoke, even if the interviewer smokes and offers you a cigarette.
- DON'T answer questions with a simple 'Yes' or 'No'. Explain wherever possible. Tell those things about yourself that relate to the position.
- DON'T lie. Answer questions truthfully, frankly and as to the point as possible.
- DON'T ever make derogatory remarks about your present or former employer. If you are unhappy with

them, try to phrase your remarks positively: 'My needs and those the company could provide were different.' Rather than: 'They didn't give me what I wanted.'

- DON'T over-answer questions. The interviewer may steer the conversation into politics or economics. As this can be tricky, answer the questions honestly but try not to say more than is necessary.
- DON'T enquire about salary, holidays, bonuses or retirement benefits at the initial interview unless you are positive the employer is interested in hiring you. However, you should know your market value and be prepared to specify your required salary or range.
- DON'T panic if there's a silence (even though it might seem like an eternity!). Take a few seconds to think about your answers. Some interviewers may use silence at the end of an answer to unnerve you. Keep calm, *smile* and wait.
- If you are asked about your weaknesses, be prepared to talk about the innocuous ones. Make the weakness relevant but not integral to the role!! Remember a weakness in relation to a job may be a skill gap. If it's obvious that in the job you are applying for some training will be required, DON'T try and avoid the issue, but deal with it head on: 'I don't have any direct experience in that area of engineering but I believe my management and commercial skills make up for that, and I learn quickly.'

Closing the interview

You have come to the end of the interview. The interviewer smiles and indicates the questions are over. Don't make the mistake and nervously mumble 'Thank You' and leave—at least not if you're interested in the position. A seasoned interviewer will normally use the closing minutes to ask if you have any questions about the job or the organisation. Don't stumble here.

Always be prepared to *ask* questions at the end of the interview—have at least one intelligent question that indicates you've been listening. This is the perfect time to introduce something that may work to your credit but hasn't yet been raised. If the interviewer doesn't give you the opportunity to keep the conversation moving, create it yourself by saying something like: 'One thing that hasn't come out in our discussion today that you might find helpful is...', or 'We seem to have covered most points about the job but there are still a few points I'd like to clarify about the company. Could you tell me...'

Of course this is also a good opportunity to let the interviewer know you are terribly keen on the job. What's the point of all that preparation and research, making it to the first interview, and being short-listed for the second interview if you don't take a proactive stance? Don't worry about appearing too eager—the company is looking for an enthusiastic employee, not someone who hasn't decided if this is the right career for them.

- If you are interested in the position, ask for it. Ask for the next interview if the situation demands. If you are offered the position, and you want it, accept on the spot. If you would like some time to think it over be courteous and tactful in asking for that time. Set a definite date for providing an answer. Be commercial and businesslike about the time frames you put on coming back to them with an answer.
- Ask for feedback. If possible, get them to give you a feel for whether they think you are a potential short-list candidate and how you rank against other candidates. Suggest that even though you are considering other positions, this one interests you the most, but you don't want to hold off on the others if it isn't going to come to anything.

- Don't be too discouraged if no definite offer is made or specific salary discussed. This does not mean you have failed to impress. Most interviewers will want to interview all the applicants before making a decision and, if it's a senior position, it's likely they will confer with their superiors before making the commitment.

- If you get the impression the interview has not gone well and you have already been rejected, don't let your enthusiasm wane. Once in a while an interviewer who is genuinely interested in your possibilities may seem to discourage you in order to test your reaction. Or they might be cautious because the other candidates have not yet been interviewed.

- As you say goodbye, you should look the interviewer in the eye and thank them for their time and for considering you for the position. If you've been interviewed by a board, thank each one individually. If they don't offer their hand, at this stage offer yours with a smile and shake hands firmly. It's likely to be the last impression you make, so you might as well appear friendly and confident. What have you got to lose?

If you have answered the two questions uppermost in the interviewer's mind—'Why are you interested in the job and the company?' and 'What can you offer and can you do the job?'—you have done all you can.

Post-interview review

If you were short-listed for this interview by a consultant it is vital that immediately after the interview you phone the consultant to report on what happened:

- if you felt you did well;
- the kinds of questions raised;
- how you handled the interviewer personally;

- the kind of response you gleaned when leaving the interview.

The consultant will want to know if you're interested in the position or not, plus what you think the company's reaction will be. Apart from obtaining a truer analysis of your prospects (after all, the consultant knows the client well, has met with them on numerous occasions and knows what they are looking for) it will also give the consultant *your* interpretation of events before the employer calls the consultant for feedback. This information will prepare the consultant to further bid on your behalf.

Naturally, if the position appears too daunting or is really not what you had in mind, you must discuss this with the consultant immediately.

Whether it seems to be the ideal job for you or not, it is important to thoroughly analyse how you performed. Before you forget what was actually discussed, list all the topics covered in the interview. Now write down the answers to the following questions:

- Had you done enough preparation?
- Did the interviewer catch you out on facts about the organisation?
- Were you relaxed and in control? Did you manage to avoid any memory blocks? Did you articulate your motivations well?
- Did you remember to smile?
- Could you have handled the interviewer better on a personal basis? Did the interviewer seem friendly and interested in you?
- Which anticipated topics actually came up for discussion?
- Did you take the opportunity to introduce some topics yourself? Which ones?

- In which elements of the interview do you feel you best performed? Where do you think you might have failed? What could you do in future to prevent that happening again?
- What questions did you find particularly difficult? How can you turn that to your advantage in the future?
- What sort of overall impression do you think you made?
- If you are called for further interviews, what aspects of your performance will you try to improve and how will you do this?

Don't wait until you know the outcome of your interview before you assess your performance—success or failure in getting the job could colour your perception. *Evaluation is important to avoid making the same mistakes again.* If you are successful in getting the job, it's still important to do the analysis. Chances are this is not the last interview you'll ever attend.

If you are declined for the job on the spot, don't get depressed. It's inevitable that many people interviewed as part of the selection process will not get jobs because more people are interviewed than there are vacancies. Keep trying. Very few people get the first or even second job they are interviewed for—even outstanding people.

If you haven't heard whether you've got the job or not, it may be that a selection hasn't yet been made. Rather than sit back and wait patiently, follow-up the interview with a letter or phone call two or three days later, enquiring about your chances of being chosen for the position. If you follow up effectively you could re-cultivate their interest in you as a candidate and show the organisation that you are a proactive person who goes after objectives with enthusiasm. A positive follow-up could be just what it takes to receive positive consideration.

If you are subsequently told you have missed out on the position (and you have thoroughly evaluated your interview and found it to be fairly faultless), pluck up your courage and contact the interviewer, preferably by phone, to ask politely what it was about your interview that let you down. This feedback can be invaluable *but your approach needs to be handled sensitively*:

- Don't put interviewers in a position where they have to justify why you weren't employed over the other candidates.
- Stress that you understand only one candidate could win the job and while you're disappointed you want to ensure you don't make the same mistakes in other interviews.
- Whatever the reason given, don't attempt to counter the interviewer's comments: 'But I'm not really like that, you just misinterpreted the situation.'
- Listen politely, then thank the interviewer for the opportunity to present your case at the interview and for the time taken in helping you assess your interview performance.

Be sure to prepare a telephone script so you come across as confident and willing to learn from your (perceived) mistakes. It could go something like this:

Applicant Good morning, Mr Jones. This is Harold Smith. You interviewed me a few weeks ago for the job as marketing manager but I haven't heard back from you. I'd like to say I'm still keen on the position with your company—is it still available?

Mr Jones Oh, thank you for your call Mr Smith. No, I'm afraid that position has been filled.

Applicant Oh, I'm sorry to hear that. At least, I'm sorry to hear I missed out as I was very keen to join your company in this role. Would you please tell me one thing, Mr Jones?

Mr Jones What is it?

Applicant I was quite pleased with the way the interview went but I realise I must have missed a vital ingredient necessary for the job. It would be most helpful in my future job interviews if you could tell me where, in your view, I went wrong.

Mr Jones Mr Smith, I was impressed with your interview and your credentials are very good. It's just that you were competing in a tough field and there was an applicant with more experience in pure marketing.

Applicant Do you think I have a chance of being employed as a marketing manager in another organisation?

Mr Jones As I said, I was very impressed with your interview and you certainly were a strong contender, you just had stronger competition. I'm sure that with your skills and attitude you should have no problem in locating a similar position with another company and I wish you all the best for your future job search.

Applicant Thank you for your time, Mr Jones. I'm delighted you were happy with the interview, and even though I missed out on this opportunity, at least I can approach the next one with confidence.

On the other hand, if you know your interview didn't go very well and you want to discover the element that alienated the interviewer, you could fashion your questions differently to discover your weaknesses. Such a conversation might go something like this:

Applicant Mr Jones, it's Harold Smith speaking. You interviewed me a few weeks ago for the advertised position of marketing manager. I'm still very keen on the job and wonder if it's still available?

Mr Jones Oh, Mr Smith. Well, yes, the position is still open but we haven't yet made a decision. In fact, we're still interviewing.

Applicant Mr Jones, since you interviewed me weeks ago, and you're still interviewing, I take it that I'm not a suitable candidate for the position?

Mr Jones Well, yes, Mr Smith, that's correct.

Applicant Obviously there were elements of my interview that failed to impress you. If you have a moment, Mr Jones, I would very much appreciate it if you could tell me a few of the areas where I may have fallen down in the interview.

Mr Jones Well, to be honest, Mr Smith, I didn't perceive you as having enough confidence to handle this position, which has a fairly high public profile. You had great difficulty in keeping eye contact when we were talking and you seemed reluctant to explain fully why you left your last position. I had the impression you were attempting to cover something up, and that attitude doesn't suit our company approach. Overall, you do appear to have excellent credentials—that's not a problem. But this position needs someone who has up-front confidence and an element of persuasion, and you just don't present yourself as being that person.

Applicant Thank you for those comments, Mr Jones. I do understand that by necessity you must make your decision on one interview. I'm afraid it's been rather a long time since I've applied for a job and I'm a little rusty on the technique. I'll certainly take the points you have made into consideration in my next interview. I haven't anything to hide about why I left my last company so I'll make sure I'm confident about that in the future.

Mr Jones I'm sorry I've had to discount you on this occasion.

Applicant Thank you very much for your time and honesty, Mr Jones. I really appreciate your constructive comments.

If your follow-up shapes up like either of these examples, take the time to write a letter to Mr Jones thanking him for taking the time to give you constructive criticism on your performance. It won't necessarily give you another shot at the job, but it will leave a good impression. Such impressions can go a lot further than the company in question. In any industry there is networking, and you could find yourself in a position where you'll be called to an interview for a similar job in another organisation. At worst, you'll have probably convinced Mr Jones that it was worth taking the effort to talk to you, and you will have gained valuable information.

The second interview

You may be called back for a second, and sometimes a third, interview. Use the same approach each time and stay alert. You should be asking more questions each time to clarify all the issues associated with the job, the company, their expectations, and yours. *Never assume you've got the job until the offer is received verbally and confirmed in writing.*

Starting off on the right foot

You've been offered the job. Congratulations!

When you receive your letter of offer, don't just sign it. Write your own letter saying how much you enjoyed the interview, how enthusiastic you are about working for such a prestigious/fast-moving/forward-thinking company. You're looking forward to starting on such and such a date. Show them you have what it takes. Confirm you *were* the best choice for the job: 'I'll be thinking a lot about this job over the next few weeks. Is there any literature you can send me on the company, any information you could provide to perhaps improve my ability to quickly absorb the duties of my role?'

Not many recipients of new jobs bother to write a letter of thanks, let alone a letter showing interest and enthusiasm for the position. The boss is already impressed and you haven't even started yet! Now all you have to do is keep up the enthusiasm and prove you are the best choice.

Positive statements or words for letters and interviews for now

In the 1970s and 1980s we often used language without thinking about what we actually conveyed. Now we need to be more aware. Here are some illustrations:

1970S & 1980S SPEAK	NOW SPEAK
I'm dogmatic.	I'm tenacious.
I'm successful.	I have achieved a lot.
I work long hours.	I'm hardworking.
I'm a people person or I like people.	I can relate well to people and they usually respond well to me.
I'm a good manager.	I can get results through people.
I dislike meetings.	I like to avoid meetings which are long and unproductive.
I'm good at selling.	I have always achieved my sales target and am regarded as persuasive.
I am a 'marketer'.	I have sound 'strategic skills' as well as salesmanship.
I can be aggressive.	I can be assertive.
I come from the school of hard knocks.	I have practical rather than theoretical experience, which I can put to use immediately.
My family always comes first.	My work and my family are equally important in achieving a balanced lifestyle. They go hand in hand.

I know a lot of people around town.	I believe I have some relevant contacts in the industry which could help me in the role you describe.
I am looking for an attractive remuneration package.	I am seeking a competitive level of remuneration commensurate with a challenging role. I recognise that part of it might be performance based.
What are the perks?	Can you break down the package for me, please?
I am not looking for a job.	I am currently employed and just in the exploratory stage at present.
What are the budgets/ sales targets?	If I am successful in getting the job, how will you measure my performance?
Does the job entail travelling?	How much travel is required to be successful in the job?
Who would I report to in the job?	Where do I fit into in the company's structure?
What are the working hours?	What expectations of working hours does your firm have?
What's my office like and do I have a secretary?	Could you describe/show me the working environment?
I can get people to do things my way.	I have persuasive skills, which I use constructively.
I am an autocrat.	I have high standards, which I expect my team to emulate.
I work hard and I play hard.	Don't say it, they'll assume the worst!

I'm told I'm pedantic.	I have an eye for detail and like to be thorough where practical.
I don't like managing people.	I prefer to work in a functional or staff role or without the daily responsibility of a team.
I don't like big companies.	I prefer to work in smaller groups or teams.
I don't like small companies.	I thrive on working within the infrastructure of a larger group or company.
I'm a straight shooter.	I like to be direct, where possible, although always sensitive to others.

THE RECRUITMENT COMPANY INTERVIEW 2

The difference between being interviewed by a recruiter, as opposed to a company, is that the recruiter often *initially* won't be interviewing you for a specific job but for a more general assessment of your abilities.

The first part of the interview will be broader and will explore various options that may not necessarily be related to the position you think you have applied for. Recruiters constantly talk to a range of candidates and their mandate is to find the best fit. They are looking for a match between your skills and the various opportunities on their books.

If you are responding directly to a company you have been able to prepare your answers about wanting to work in that industry, in a particular job. When you go to a recruitment consultant you usually don't have the benefit of knowing about the company, so you need to understand that the questions being fielded will be more general.

Most professional recruiters do not reveal the identity of the client until such time as they have evaluated the candidate's background and motivation (unless, of course, the client has stipulated that their name and logo appear in the advertisement). Remember, there are a great many talented people around who have the right answers—but what do they really want to do in life? A consultant might be interviewing an accountant who really wants to be a salesperson. That's why most recruitment companies start with the *preference side* of the interview.

BE PREPARED FOR QUESTIONS ALONG THESE LINES:

- What are you looking for in the future?
- What sort of company would you like to work for?
- Which industry preferences do you have?
- Where do you want to live?
- Why are you exploring other options?
- Who had the greatest impact on your life?
- Describe your mentors of the past.

If you say your mentor is a parent, for example, and you describe them as people who never allow obstacles to get in the way of attaining their goals, you are describing your alter ego, you are describing a significant source of influence on you and your likely response to similar situations. On that basis you are revealing a lot to the interviewer.

While such questions might appear to be obtuse, it's important to listen, then answer as openly and honestly as you can. Remember to stay alert, and try to anticipate what the next question will be.

THE COMPETENCY/ BEHAVIOURAL-BASED INTERVIEW

Behavioural interviewing is a technique that has been around for a number of years and it is relatively easy to detect someone who has been trained in it.

The questions asked in a behavioural interview are designed to elicit from candidates how they have behaved in the past, as opposed to what they would do or what they think. *It is based on the principle that you can predict future performance on the basis of past performance.*

If an interviewer is looking for someone who is 'results oriented' they will probably ask a question like: 'Give me an example of an occasion when you achieved your goal, against all the odds.' Once the response is given, they could ask further questions such as: 'What were the challenges? How did you overcome them?'

Because the behavioural interviewers are looking for *evidence* of behaviour, they are not just listening for what the interviewees have done, but also *how* they went about it.

In some instances behavioural interviewing has become more sophisticated as the result of organisations doing competency analysis on roles before recruiting for them. In brief: competency analysis identifies the skills, knowledge and attributes required for someone to be successful in a position in that organisation. Because the interviewer has a clearly defined 'benchmark' to interview against, they can be far more probing in their behavioural interviewing.

Whilst it may sound a little intimidating to interviewees who have not been through a competency-based interview, the feedback from those who have been exposed to this technique has been extremely positive. They generally feel that the interviews are very focused and have given them a real opportunity to talk about their relevant skills, rather than talk generalities which is often the case in unstructured interviews.

When involved in a behavioural or competency-based interview, *do not make sweeping statements*—give clear examples that prove why you have a particular skill or attribute. The interviewer will not accept that you think you are a good leader, they want specific examples which *prove* you are a good leader, ie. an example where your leadership made the difference between success and failure in a particular situation or event.

4 APPLYING FOR JOBS IN THE PUBLIC SECTOR

The rules for applying for jobs in the public sector are very different from the techniques which apply in the private sector. The most significant difference is the way the application is written and the structure of the interview.

Behind every position advertised, there is a selection committee of three to four people. This committee is responsible for screening the applications in accordance with the *essential and desirable criteria* for the position—as stated in the advertisement. If your application does not demonstrate how you meet these criteria it is very unlikely you will be granted an interview.

The application

Before putting an application together, it is important you ring the contact person named in the advertisement. They will send you a package of information on the job and organisation and the application form; and, if required, be available to answer any questions you may have about the position.

You shouldn't think of an application for a public sector job as a résumé, but as an application form with a series of attachments. Where the private sector usually requires only a covering letter and résumé, the public sector requires:

- covering letter;
- completed official application form;
- information addressing the essential and desirable criteria;
- educational history;
- work history;
- additional information;
- referees.

The covering letter, educational history, work history, additional information and referees should all be written in the same way that you would present information in the private sector.

Fill in the personal data on the application form and sign it, but write 'see attached' across all other sections relating to work history. *Do not fall into the trap of trying to squeeze your life history on to the application form.*

The most critical part of the application is the section covering *essential and desirable criteria.* Under each criterion you should list all your relevant work experience, skills and achievements which demonstrate how you meet that criterion. Try to be as specific as possible. For example, in answer to 'Demonstrate a high level of communication skills', it is not sufficient to state that you were required to use a high level of communication skills in your last two positions. You should aim to show as much detail of depth and breadth of experience as is relevant:

Over the last five years in the capacity of (marketing manager) I frequency had to communicate with people on the shop floor right up to the level of CEO. Communication was in the form of written reports and I was also responsible for ...

When providing the names of at least two *referees*, be aware that any existing written references you have will probably not be considered, and it is possible that the referee will be asked to reply to set questions in writing.

The interview

The philosophy behind a public sector interview is 'the best person for the job', based on the selection criteria (essential and desirable). There are very strict guidelines set down, which must be followed by the selection committee. *The most important one to be aware of is that questions asked at the interview must be based on the advertised criteria.* Also, the same set of questions must be asked of each person being interviewed.

The average interview time for a public sector interview is 20–40 minutes, and it is rare for there to be more than one interview. The panel may decide, however, to base the final selection on the written application as well as the interview.

PSYCHOLOGICAL APPRAISAL—ORDEAL OR OPPORTUNITY?

The job interview went smoothly, they seem to like you and you like them. Then they throw you a curly one: 'Would you mind having a psychological appraisal?'

There is no surer way of striking fear and outrage into the hearts of many job candidates than to ask them to undergo psychological appraisal. But before taking umbrage, consider the positive side. Whatever the results, you can use them to your advantage. You'll gain valuable insights into your personality and your potential abilities. And you can use the information to help steer your career and your life in a profitable and personally satisfying direction.

As more employers use psychological testing to help select new employees and evaluate existing ones, it may be helpful to dispel some of the fears and myths associated with them.

Psychological testing is done to minimise a costly job mismatch, which is enormously important both to the employer and to you, the candidate. It is demoralising to end up in a position that is not right for you, so try to approach the testing with a positive frame of mind. This way you will be minimising the possibility of making a disastrous career move.

The battery of tests usually falls into two major groups: *tests of ability* and *personality tests*. The tests of ability are designed to illuminate a person's capabilities in a range of different areas, while the personality tests are a way of gaining insight into characteristics that may not be readily volunteered at an interview.

Tests of ability

These cover numeracy, critical thinking, verbal comprehension and reasoning, logical and analytical thinking, problem-solving and general intelligence. Additional specific exercises may be included to suit the requirements of a particular job.

The tests require a combination of speed and accuracy and look at how people respond to problem-solving in an environment that has the added pressure of time.

Personality tests

These are more complicated to interpret and are sometimes maligned for a number of reasons:

- Some questions appear ridiculous: 'I have strange and peculiar thoughts' or 'Evil spirits possess me at times'. A person who is not well adjusted *can* identify with these questions.
- Some may not seem relevant: 'When I am with people I am bothered by hearing very queer things', or 'Once a week or more often I suddenly feel hot all over, without apparent cause'. Here, the tests are looking at groupings of questions, not individual items.
- Personality tests are sometimes misused. We often hear complaints from candidates who did not receive any feedback or were told they had been rejected on the basis of their psychological results. People who 'fail' these tests are justifiably mystified: 'Don't I have a personality?'
- Sometimes the tests are interpreted by people who do not have a great deal of experience or understanding of the subtleties of the results.

A candidate's guide to assessment centres

While the most common type of 'selection activity' is the interview, increasingly employers are using other activities to assess the extent of the 'job–person' fit. This section is designed to introduce you to different types of selection activities.

Individual exercises

APTITUDE TESTS

These are typically timed activities, where you are required to read a question and provide an answer as quickly and accurately as possible. Aptitude tests are generally paper and pencil tests, but can also be done at the computer. They can assess such things as word comprehension, numerical reasoning aptitude, mathematical aptitude, spatial reasoning aptitude, and so on. The type of test used will depend on the job itself.

Example: You may be given a table of numbers which have been incorrectly added up. Your job may be to identify and correct the errors that have been made.

IN-TRAYS

An in-tray (or in-basket) exercise involves you working from the contents of someone's in-tray—reading general information, memos, letters, invoices or documents in order to make decisions and action items, balancing the volume of work against a tight timetable.

Example: You may be asked to act in the role of a manager, who is planning the set-up of a shared service centre. Your tasks would be based around organising the centre, covering issues to do with personnel, IT and finance.

PERSONALITY, MOTIVATION AND INTEREST QUESTIONNAIRES

These are generally known as 'self report' questionnaires. They can be administered by computer or in a paper and pencil format and are untimed. You should answer in an honest and straightforward manner as there are no right or wrong answers. The questionnaires are designed to assess your interpersonal style, work style, achievement drive, motivators and interests at work.

Example: You will be required to select the most appropriate or suitable response out of a range of multiple-choice answers to each question. Questions may relate to your preferred decision-making style, how you relate to others, your preferred/favourite activities at work, etc.

Interactive exercises

GROUP EXERCISES

Group exercises are timed discussions, where a group of participants work together to tackle a particular problem. You are observed by assessors, who are not looking for right or wrong answers, but for how you interact with your colleagues in the team.

Example: You may be assigned to a special task force, investigating how customer service standards can be improved within a hotel chain. You may each have different views about how the service can best be improved, and you may need to reach consensus on the best way to move forward.

PRESENTATIONS

You may be required to make a formal presentation about a particular topic to a group of assessors. In some cases you may be given time to prepare, in other cases you may be required to 'think on your feet'.

INTERVIEWS

Traditional interviews are likely to include a review of your education, training, previous work history and interests. Structured interviews are more likely to require you to give examples of how you have demonstrated a skill or personal attribute in the past which is pertinent to the role you are applying for.

Example: You may be required to describe a time where you have demonstrated teamwork.

How to do your best in a psychological test

Get a good night's sleep. If you've been out raising hell the night before you'll probably perform badly.

Consult the various books available which illuminate the structure of the tests and types of problems you may be required to solve.

Determine the time of day when you are at your peak performance. We work on the assumption that people are fresher earlier in the day, but if you are not a 'morning person', request another time.

Stay calm and relaxed (easier said than done, we know), as extreme anxiety can adversely affect your performance. Deep breathing can be helpful as it forces you to slow down. Avoid caffeine as it exacerbates the jittery feeling associated with nervousness.

If you are anxious, or something happening in your life is causing you concern, tell the psychologist during your pre-assessment interview. The more knowledge they have of your state of mind, the better able they are to make an accurate assessment of the results.

During the pre-assessment interview the psychologist should explain what the tests are designed to do: why you are undergoing them, and what happens to the results. If you have concerns or questions, don't be afraid to raise them.

Try to avoid assessing yourself as you go. Many of the tests are difficult to finish within the prescribed time, and you'll increase your anxiety and decrease your performance by worrying. *Stop thinking your future hinges on your performance in these tests—it doesn't.*

Be honest. There are good reasons why you shouldn't say what you don't really believe is true:

- You may invalidate the test (or come up as very strange). Good psychological tests have an effective validation key that picks up inconsistencies and reveals when someone is trying to appear too good to be true.
- The organisation may not have a definite idea of what they want in terms of personality.

- You may be inaccurate in your assessment of their needs.

Testing can work to your advantage:

- If you lack formal qualifications but do well on the tests of abilities. You have an opportunity to prove yourself intellectually capable of the demands of the job.
- If you are a brilliant student but lack the specific skills required for the job. In this case you would probably be dissatisfied with the role.
- If the employer feels that your personality may not fit in. Chances are you would not be happy working there.

Use the feedback session to glean as much information as you can for your own career development. The appraisal can assess where your skills and abilities fit. Ask the psychologist for ideas on areas for improvement, or discuss your personal aspirations in the light of results.

The main issue to bear in mind when undergoing psychological appraisal is that it will ultimately work for you. Use the opportunity to explore your potential and take control of your career direction.

6 SALARY PACKAGES

Negotiating your offer

The biggest single change in remuneration compensation over the past ten years has been the move towards performance-based salary packages where an organisation might offer an employee a $100 000 package comprising $70 000 basic salary and $30 000 based on performance, ie. 70 per cent salary and 30 per cent 'at risk' incentive.

You should not, however, become confused by the fact that a minority of very senior and high-profile chief executives have suddenly received significant increases in remuneration, irrespective of the performance of their company. This is explained by the fact that Australia needed to catch up with the rest of the world in salaries paid to CEOs of medium- and large-sized companies.

In many other areas, particularly middle to senior management, executive compensation has plateaued. Indeed, a number of organisations have not only frozen salary packages outside productivity performance increases, but have actually reduced salary packages in some areas.

As the restructuring and recovery of our economy takes place, there will be a gradual resumption of annual salary increases. Working on the assumption that low inflation is here to stay, increases will be based on merit and performance rather than standard across-the-board percentage increases which were the hallmark of the 1970s and 1980s.

The introduction of fringe benefits tax (FBT) changed salary packages considerably. In the past, large corporations offered an extensive menu of fringe benefits which were, in practice, 100 per cent tax effective. But as FBT moved in on these perks we have seen the emergence of the 'cost to company' salary package.

While FBT was designed to be paid by employers, increasingly, if an employee has chosen to take fringe benefits as part of the package, the FBT cost is passed on to the employee. The benefits are grossed up and a total cost to the company worked out, which includes a cash component, the FBT, and in some cases the tax on the FBT itself. More companies are now moving towards this form of 'cost to company' remuneration.

The big move is towards performance-based bonuses. These will flow down through the organisation. Employees not traditionally recipients of a bonus such as the shop floor, non-sales or marketing personnel, and administration, will also see some element of their package based on the performance of the company, their department, and/or quantitative and qualitative performance factors related to their own jobs.

Bonus schemes are obviously attractive for the reason that they have a great deal of flexibility. They free companies to pay for performance while not locking them in to hefty salary packages. At the same time, any reduction of the top tax rate means that more money actually goes into the recipients' pockets.

Combined with an incentive scheme, this greater flexibility could be enough to attract some employees, even though the up-front cost has not gone up at all. There is a big tip here for competitive and contemporary employers when trying to attract new employees. The really smart ones are also incorporating 'participation' schemes where employees benefit if the company's capital value increases, either via real or phantom equity schemes. A great deal of new ground in 'Reward Systems' will be covered in the next five years.

The golden triangle

Golden Handshakes, or Golden Hellos, as they are often called, may still exist in some areas. This is basically the process of buying a promised bonus that might be lost if an employee moves to a new company. Or for someone outstanding, it is a pure cash incentive to join, a bit like a transfer fee for a professional football player.

Golden Hellos can also act as Golden Handcuffs, as the payment is often tied to a minimum length of service or it has to be repaid!

Other handcuffs include share options schemes and bonus payments that are partly paid upon receipt and partly deferred over time, so a residue of benefits builds up which can act as a disincentive to leave.

For most of us mere mortals, Golden Hellos or Golden Handcuffs will not be part of the package, but a Golden Parachute might be.

If you believe you are making a major career decision that cuts across a totally different area, and particularly if you are being wooed to leave your present employer, you might want a Golden Parachute: a longer notice period (up to two years), or some other cash benefit in case, for some reason, this new career move does not work. Careful negotiation will be required here, as it is possible for the job offer to fall through at this delicate stage.

However, if you are not being wooed and you are not currently employed, or if it is a job that you really want, then a Golden Parachute is unlikely to be a significant part of the negotiation process.

Negotiating the actual offer

In many cases the basic salary being offered for a position will be stipulated up front, either in the advertisement or by the recruitment consultant. If the figure is open to negotiation make sure you know before the interview what you are prepared to accept. As the interview unwinds, send out signals about the sort of remuneration you are looking for. At the same time, try to detect what they are offering. Hopefully the two are on track.

If there is a significant gap between what you are expecting and what the employer is prepared to pay then something has gone wrong earlier on in the recruitment process. If the offer matches your expectations, accept it on the spot. Don't play hard to get. If you need time for some reason then simply say 'yes in principle' but you'd like a few days to think things through carefully.

If you are called back for a second interview, at that stage it is certainly appropriate to clarify what sort of income you are looking for and what the firm is prepared to pay.

What am I worth?

In terms of measuring your skills in the current market, find out what people with similar skills in similar industries or jobs are earning: does it fit in with your own income aspirations?

If you are making a move to a totally new industry or career, you may have to take a step backwards before you resume your upward path in terms of income. How can you possibly be worth what you were earning before, if in the new company your skills and attributes are not going to be fully productive for the first three, six or even twelve months?

Ultimately you will know what you are worth by measuring it against what people are prepared to pay for your services. It's like the family home. What's it worth today? What someone is prepared to pay for it today!

Contracts

Most companies will offer a contract of employment these days which will stipulate the basic terms and conditions of employment. There are still a number of firms that do this in a brief letter form, which is not necessarily a bad thing—depending on the track record of that organisation and the success of the people who have joined it in the past.

THE LETTER OF CONTRACT SHOULD SPECIFY:

- the nature of the job;
- the remuneration in total package terms;
- other benefits, such as a bonus and non-packaged items (if any);

- annual leave;
- the terms and conditions of termination including reasons and notice period.

Some companies have a confidentiality agreement which covers sensitive information: their intellectual property, and that of their customers.

Contracts of employment are a complex area. If you have specific concerns you should seek your own legal advice. For 95 per cent of cases, a letter merely clarifies the details of the job, the terms, the conditions, and the exit methodologies. If you feel it is adequate then it is probably the way to go.

RESIGNING WITH DIGNITY

You've accepted your new job. Now you have to resign from your current position. It might not be easy. You may be faced with the prospect of leaving a company where you've been happy, having to tell people you have known and respected for many years that you are resigning.

Or you might have loathed every minute of your working life there and can't wait to give them the flick.

You may experience the classic Cold-feet Syndrome: doubts about your ability to handle the new position; whether you'll enjoy your new environment, the people, the company culture.

The counter-offer

Your present employer may make a counter-offer—greater remuneration or increased responsibility. This is a tough one to handle, but keep in mind it shouldn't have taken the threat of your leaving before you were offered a better reward.

Do them the courtesy of listening to what they have to say, but then be firm and resilient and confirm your departure date. The counter-offer might drag on for weeks, which could delay your departure and jeopardise your new job.

If the offer is too good to refuse, make sure you don't accept it without analysing what led you to look for an alternative job in the first place.

TO RESIGN WITH DIGNITY THERE ARE A FEW BASIC RULES:

- Don't quibble about the things you perceived were wrong with the company.
- Don't criticise your boss, even if you could truthfully do so.
- Don't make your present colleagues feel inadequate by comparing your old job with the new one.
- Leave the organisation without burning any bridges.

The best approach, and one that could be adopted almost universally, is to meet your boss personally and say something along the lines of:

I've really enjoyed my time with your organisation and I believe this company and your management team have taught me a great deal, but for reasons related to my own career aspirations I have uncovered an opportunity that is too good for me to pass up. It's really not a question of leaving here because I'm disgruntled in any way. It's more to do with a need to move on, to spread my wings. I need a change and the new job offers me certain advancements I don't believe I can get from this organisation.

After explaining your reasons for leaving, follow-up with a formal letter.

DEVELOPING YOUR CAREER

Well, you got the job. Of all the candidates interviewed, analysed, put through the wringer—*as a result of your well-planned search!*—you came up trumps. *Don't sit back on your laurels—this is the beginning of a new chapter—not an end in itself.*

Before taking up your new position write a letter of thanks to your new boss expressing your enthusiasm and interest in your new career. That will certainly distinguish you from the crowd and create a positive impression— before you've even started!

Having achieved your goal, don't forget those who helped along the way—friends, mentors, consulting firms, other employers, or personnel people who set you on the right path. Take the time to write a personal note of thanks. Knowing you've been placed will also vindicate their belief in you. And it would be foolish not to, as you might need them again in the future.

Never underestimate the network of executives in an industry. If it gets back to your new employer that you sent a personal note of thanks to another potential employer, it will confirm you were a good choice.

The way you strategically come to grips with your new job will actually dictate the next few years of your career with the company. Long after their apprenticeship is over, some employees are still seen by senior management as the young, untrained person who arrived for their first day of work many years before. This is not necessarily the case— *it is simply a warning*. Once your superiors form their perceptions about your ability they will be hard to change. If your firm doesn't have a performance appraisal system, such notions will be even more difficult to shake.

EARLY DAYS

Here are a few tips to consolidate your credibility.

- The first weeks in any job involve a lot of introductions. Ask for an organisational chart or note down each person's name as you are introduced. If you have time before meeting your new colleagues, ask your boss to tell you their names, positions and duties, so you can instantly place each one in the context of their position in the organisation. Quickly learning who your co-workers are and what they do will facilitate the cooperation that is necessary for you to come to grips with your job.

- Focus immediately on familiarising yourself with the basics of the job. If it's appropriate, make notes—it's better to have more information than less. Your new employer may become irritated if information has to be constantly repeated.

- Establish with your boss your priorities over the next three-, six- and twelve-month periods. Many employers may not be prepared for this and they will be suitably impressed. More importantly, it will reaffirm discussions at the interview stage in terms of expectations of you and your performance. Many talented executives come a cropper when they fail to understand the real expectations of their employers. Often minor issues can be resolved before they reach an impasse and a situation where the relationship breaks down.

- Ask your boss for recommendations as to your role over the first few weeks. This ensures there is absolutely no doubt in anyone's mind what you should be doing before you come to grips with the ebb and flow of the business. *This is a vital step.* Many talented new employees have been left to vegetate by bosses who assume they are 'getting on with things'. If the rot sets in, it's really difficult to correct—even at this early stage.

- Set up a meeting with each of your new colleagues just to get to know them. This will help clarify exactly what they do in the organisation and where your job fits in with theirs—what the overlap is and the cooperation you will require. You will quickly gain a better insight into their personality and accelerate friendship and cooperation.

- Make sure you acquaint yourself with your colleagues' correct names, the spelling, their correct title, and their preference for being referred to either by their first name or Mr/Mrs/Ms. Some people have very firm opinions about the way they're addressed.

- Try to get a feel for the culture and politics of the organisation—where the power bases lie, and what the unwritten rules are. For instance, you might discover that you should never park your car in the sales manager's spot—even if it's pouring with rain and it's only for three minutes. Solicit advice from your colleagues. Many pitfalls can be avoided just by asking intelligent questions.

- If you feel your old company did things better, desist from making comparisons—it will only antagonise your co-workers. *When you've established your position,* and you assess the moment is right, you can suggest innovations that may make the organisation function better.

- Observe who the movers and shakers of the company are by reading staff magazines, watching who constantly pops up on staff videos, and reading noticeboards. Read the internal telephone directory and familiarise yourself with their positions and those of their subordinates.

- If they haven't made the first move, introduce yourself to others in the organisation. Do anything that will help to establish you as a friendly person in the company. It will make you a happier employee, which is good, because happy, accepted employees are productive and successful.

2 COMPANY POLITICS—CULTURE AND UNWRITTEN RULES

Politicking goes on in most organisations. Employees from all levels jockey for every opportunity to make a good impression, to outdo their colleagues—anything that will give them the edge for future promotion.

Many believe that in this competitive world a ruthless approach is the only way. But often, if they get to the top, their positions are insecure. There are people who would be more than gleeful to see them fall—and do everything in their power to make that happen.

Smart, successful people follow the old adage: Be nice to everyone you meet on the way up, because they are the ones you might be meeting on your descent. Don't burn your bridges. You often have no idea who will be useful to you in your career—supporters can come from the most unlikely places—so it's best to combine your ambition and desire to get on with a generous, courteous and helpful approach. It will ensure you're a *real* winner.

But how do you cope when you come up against a 'make-it-at-any-cost' co-worker?

- Ensure your tasks are completed in an exemplary manner—your work is accurate, efficient, effective and proactive. Never attempt to lessen your attention at work in favour of meeting your antagonist on the same dirty turf—you might just get beaten and you won't have a solid leg to stand on.
- Use a safety valve. When you get a new assignment, either have your boss put it in writing, or *you* write a note confirming your new task, the initial research and the proposed expectations. If possible, have your superior sign it as a confirmation. You're likely to be seen as an organised, dedicated, interested worker—a belief that will stand you in good stead in the future.

Always approach fellow workers, especially those in positions further down the rung from you, with cheerfulness and courtesy. Some people, when they reach senior positions, treat subordinates discourteously, rudely ordering them to carry out menial duties. *This is a very bad move.* The younger, less-experienced staff are usually listened to by the boss if there are any problems in the office. On a purely personal basis, you know it's the wrong approach. Remember when you were the junior? And you never know who your superior will be tomorrow. Your treatment of subordinates may very well determine the course of your future career.

But what if you want to ignore all this politicking and simply improve your position within the ranks of the organisation?

Apart from achieving the immediate objectives of your job you must start to think strategically about your career— your interrelationship with the dynamics of the organisation; where you want to be in the next two, four or six years; and what you have to do to get there.

Putting yourself in the limelight

It's important to control where you're going and not just slave over a hot job where you receive little recognition. As one writer so amusingly put it, if you simply keep your head down with your nose to the grindstone, the only thing to happen will be the removal of your nose. In other words, while hard workers are very often appreciated, they are not necessarily promoted. You have to be active in controlling your career path. To do this you must:

- *Positively demonstrate your skills* by not only working in the job outlined, but also taking on extra work. Offer assistance to your colleagues and subordinates—but be smart about it. There's no point in sharing your expertise so that someone else can take the credit. Subtly let the powers that be know it was your assistance on a certain project that helped get it in by the deadline.
- *Offer assistance to your supervisor* if and when it seems appropriate. By staying back late or working on the

weekend you'll be appreciated—and you will have planted a seed of promotion.

- *Network in the company.* Don't be a passive employee when it comes to socialising. Join the social club, squash club or the company's wine appreciation society. Eat lunch in the cafeteria and sit with different groups to discover what's happening in other areas of the organisation. Being seen as part of the team will help the company head put a face to the name when it comes to promotion time.

- *Develop a mentor in the organisation.* High achievers need to keep learning. Good performance, with or without additional development courses, isn't enough to grow to your full potential. The best learning will come from being tutored in the finer points of the job and the organisational politics.

- *Develop a yearly 'learning' plan.* Don't wait for someone to send you on a course. Be proactive about learning new skills. Find out what's available and request approval to attend. If academic qualifications are the only true path up the managerial ladder, don't feel you're too old to learn. As a mature-age student you'll have a greater breadth of life-knowledge on which to draw than your younger counterparts. Whatever path you take, demonstrate you place great importance on personal growth and development.

- *Become active in the community.* You'll find it personally satisfying and it's likely to provide valuable management expertise.

- *Join professional associations.* Apart from being prime areas in which to network with like-minded individuals, professional associations allow you to become known as a professional in your field. Is your company a member of the relevant association in Australia? What does it take to become an associate member? If you're female, why not join Women & Management? If your particular association has a newsletter, why not write an article for it? It will increase your perceived competence and expertise and demonstrate that you are creative and ambitious.

- *Develop and define clear career goals.* It's not good enough to have outlined a career path a decade ago and now be treading water while waiting for it to come to fruition. Often career goals need refinement because, as you've matured, so have your ambitions. Review your career path—ascertain where you are now and where you want to go next. Identify a position in your present company in which you'd like to be and work towards it. Whenever you're given a chance, subtly mention how keen you are to reach that position.

- *If your organisation doesn't offer you a future,* plan which job you want and where you'd like to work. Do you have the necessary skills? No? Then now is the time to develop them. Define your career goals into stages. Where do you see yourself in a year's time? What are your options?

Actively planning your career takes ambition, determination and perseverance. Don't for a moment think you can sit back and take it easy. If you do, you'll be falling behind.

GETTING RECOGNITION FOR FURTHER TRAINING

Selection for further training will come from three main opportunities. The first is the formal or informal performance appraisal where you plant the seed in your employer's mind that if the company invests time and money in further education it will enhance your performance, enabling you to make a greater contribution to the company. To succeed you will have to demonstrate that you are worth the investment by performing better than average in your present job. However, if you believe your performance is below average *because* you lack the specific training, then you have a special case and you should make it strongly. Another option to gain recognition for further training—perhaps even a one-year paid MBA at Harvard—relates to your strategic career plans. We would have to assume your performance was above average in your present role and that the organisation has already intimated you have 'potential for further promotion'.

In order to create the catalyst:

- Convey to your present employer that you can be spared for one to twelve months, depending on the nature of the training. This is important because you'll have to set up your department so well it can be run without you, or find alternative executives to carry the load.
- Persuade them your above-average performance will immediately be further enhanced by this additional training.
- Have the hallmarks of someone who is both prepared to make a long-term commitment and to rise to the next two or three levels within the company.

- Do something that is well above the call of normal duty in relation to an innovation or an idea; volunteering for additional responsibilities or duties on a one-off basis; or perhaps just pulling off that outstanding deal. While congratulations are flowing, make your move. Suggest you are really happy with the company and see your future as long-term, but you feel you need to gain specific skills in order to continue making progress.

The final and most common reason for an employer investing in you by way of further training will be brought about by change. Yes, organisational change—where jobs have been merged due to downsizing and retrenchments; change due to the introduction of new technology; and change in the way the business operates when the competition takes a new tack.

PERFORMANCE APPRAISAL

Some organisations have formalised performance appraisal systems. This is simply a situation where the boss and a subordinate sit down together, usually for a couple of hours once or twice a year, in order to:

- discuss specific achievements, strengths, weaknesses, and to review failures;
- decide what the company needs to do to provide further training to enable the employee to move on in the organisation;
- give the employee the opportunity to present the boss with some feedback on the job and the company; and,

if there are frustrations, how they could be reduced or negated—to engender a positive effect on performance.

The idea of these meetings is that they are positive and constructive. They give both parties an opportunity to openly and frankly discuss where everyone is headed. *It's important to take them seriously.*

- Prepare for the meeting by making notes about what you want to say in regard to your achievements; and your objectives for further input through training.
- Handling the appraisal well will probably involve some form of self-evaluation, so work out how you analyse your own strengths and weaknesses and be prepared to articulate that to your boss.
- If you want to raise issues which frustrate you about the way you are being managed, prepare them concisely and diplomatically. Listen carefully and put the ball back in the other court now and again by asking what your boss thinks of you and your performance in certain areas and where there is room for improvement.
- Accept constructive criticism—don't get defensive. No one is perfect. If you're without fault, you stop learning. 'If you're green you grow! If you're "ripe" you rot.' You don't ever want to be perfect (ripe).
- Finally, you need to gain commitment from your employer in terms of what the company is prepared to do towards developing your skills—and, therefore, accelerate your promotion.

If your employer doesn't have a formal appraisal scheme, ask your boss to set aside an hour or so, once a year, to discuss your performance and where your career is heading, so you can consistently strive to meet the company's objectives.

Many organisations have introduced 360 degree performance appraisal systems. This is where input about your performance is sought by subordinates, peers and superiors in the organisation. Avoid making statements when receiving feedback like 'Oh, I know who said that'.

Take valid criticism on board, learn from the feedback and strive to make changes where necessary. The idea behind 360 degree feedback is that it relies on how you get along with equals and how you manage downwards and upwards.

5 THE INTERNAL PROMOTION INTERVIEW

In some companies internal promotions are made after fairly formal interviews with one or two people present, or sometimes a panel. In other situations, you are simply observed over weeks or months, then the boss calls you in for a chat over a drink after work and discusses your aspirations and future opportunities.

In any event, such interviews certainly can't be taken for granted. They should receive the same preparation as the interview you went through to get the job:

- You have to identify, either formally or informally, which job you are being considered for, and whether or not you are interested.
- If you want the job then you have to decide the skills and training you will need in order to do it well.
- If relocation is an issue, you have to decide whether you are prepared to move for career development. Discuss it in advance with your family so you can make your commitment without hesitation once your boss has made the offer, or you are accepted.

- You must decide on fair and equitable remuneration for the new job and prepare your negotiating strategy accordingly.

At the interview, be formal. Shake hands with everybody and conduct yourself as though you are taking the whole thing very seriously. Be alert and enthusiastic.

Ask as many questions as you can. You will impress far more by asking intelligent questions about activity, expectations and the nature of the business/division/role for which you are being considered, than by sitting back and letting them do all the work.

Following the interview, ask for feedback and an indication as to whether you might be successful. Intimate that if you are in the running, you are keen and very hopeful they will give you the opportunity to demonstrate your abilities in your prospective new role.

Don't wait for weeks for someone to get back to you— follow-up on how the decision-making process is going. Put subtle pressure on them. Often the candidate who quietly follows up is the one who gets the job. This constant follow-up is interpreted as enthusiasm and application and a real hunger for the opportunity.

Employers sometimes deal tentatively with organisational promotion and this leads to ambitious employees feeling dissatisfied, which in turn has them seeking recognition and new rewards outside their own company. If you are reasonably content in your job but would like to pursue a more aggressive career path with improvements to benefits, perhaps you should persuade your boss to consider you for a bigger job when it comes up.

Lateral career moves

Instead of moving from your current company for more money and a bigger title, these days we are seeing a lot of lateral career moves within the same organisation which complement your skills and stretch you in a different way, but where the salary package might stay the same. You may move from a *project*-oriented job which uses little technology and doesn't involve the management of people, to another job which is *process*-oriented, involving high technology and management of people.

Approach the transitional job interview as though you were applying for the job as an outsider. Go through the same steps as during an internal promotion interview but remember that your questions and motives for getting this job are different. There's no more money or promotion here. Instead, it's *the opportunity to learn new skills* and that will eventually lead to a promotion down the track.

6 THE TALL POPPY SYNDROME

You may have been one of a number of people in your department—and now suddenly you have been promoted to be their boss. How do you cope with this situation and what actions do you take?

As you gradually move into your new role, gently assert your authority as you go. Then continue to do what you obviously did to get promoted—demonstrate that you are head and shoulders above the rest of your team by virtue of your performance and ability. In other words, lead by example—'do as I do, not as I say' will go down extremely well. You will probably be surprised, but your peers already have respect for your abilities and talents—they just need reassurance that as their team leader you will help them be even more successful. To put them at ease:

- inform them that you will hold weekly meetings to facilitate communication;
- let them know that you don't want them to feel alienated in any way and you don't want them to start changing the way they have always approached you;
- reassure them you need their support;
- reinforce that along with the authority, you must also bear the responsibility.

If there are a couple of individuals in the team who are obvious troublemakers, you will need to speak to them separately. Take them to one side and explain that your new job is difficult enough without their disruptions; that you would appreciate their support because they are clearly (even if they are not) among the more talented members of the team. If that fails, indicate that you have run out of patience, as they are impacting on team performance. Either they improve or steps for their dismissal will be taken. This is a last resort and must be done discreetly, constructively, and on a one-to-one basis.

Finally, you can solicit the services of your boss to help get your team behind you. Your success will probably reflect on your boss, who should be more than willing to assist you in the formative months of your new role.

ENHANCING YOUR VISIBILITY

As we've indicated all through the book, the world belongs to those people who are always thinking ahead, and who are strategic about their careers. Our observation of successful people is that they do this naturally, without having to think.

They are always visible—doing that little bit extra. *You* can orchestrate and emulate this behaviour.

This means undertaking considered and consistent action over a period of two to five years, to increase the probability of someone phoning one day, after noticing your public achievements, and requesting your attendance at an interview to discuss an exciting new career opportunity.

You have to promote yourself in order to get noticed. Modestly hiding your talents under a bushel will do nothing for your career prospects:

- Take a more active role in your profession or industry association—it will create an impression if you are a spokesperson. People who are considered successful by their peers and competitors are talked about by the industry more than anyone else. When a journalist or a headhunter, or indeed anyone else, seeks information about that industry, they're going to hear *your* name.
- On behalf of your company, come up with public relations concepts that will indirectly cause you to be quoted in the media as the author.
- Develop your public speaking skills so that when you are asked to make a presentation, you don't lack the confidence to accept, and when you do give that speech, no matter how small, you do it so well you are invited back again and again.

If you are approached by someone to discuss an opportunity, always go for a chat. What have you got to lose? If nothing else, you might learn something about the marketplace in which you are operating, and often you may find that something which sounded completely uninteresting turns out to be very special.

After the interview, if you don't wish to proceed, don't burn your bridges by (arrogantly) giving the interviewer a tough time—just because they invited you in! Such behaviour won't serve your future career interests.

If a headhunter asks you, as a source, to assist on a particular search, be cooperative. By getting close to that particular consultant you may well be considered for something else further down the track when *you* are in need of a career change.

Finally, the best way to get noticed is, of course, by producing *results* that recommend you. Then you'll always be sought out for new opportunities.

OPTIONS AND STRATEGIES

The prediction that companies would be run by an essential core of permanent staff accessing outsiders only when the need arises has now become a reality. As we mentioned earlier, many companies outsource those functions which are not core businesses, such as accounting, computing, photocopying, advertising, legal work, office cleaning and plant maintenance. For special projects a pool of temporary talent can be called upon—consultants, contractors, 'ideas people' and part-time workers. Whether it's working for the company itself when special needs arise, or handling peak loads of activity for the firm that has taken over the outsourced function, in today's world of work *being your own boss* is a most viable option.

People in full-time jobs are working longer hours than ever before and many are stepping off the traditional career path to explore new and more flexible ways of working. Some of these include:

- starting a consulting practice in their area of expertise;
- starting a small business;
- choosing a second career that, while using their skills, is dramatically different from their previous position;
- part-time work;
- working on a 'contract' basis;
- portfolio work—a mix of different jobs at any one time.

OPTIONS

Executive contracting—a form of 'outsourcing'

With changing economic pressures and new management attitudes a number of people are choosing freelancing as a career. For those executives seeking variety, stimulus, challenge and a more flexible lifestyle, this may be the answer.

In the age of lean and mean, the need for organisations to slim down and remain flexible has created the demand for contract executives with specific skills to handle specific problems. Morgan & Banks have over 4000 contract executives out on assignments weekly who are employed by clients on a project basis. There are other specialist agencies which do the same, particularly in accounting, engineering and information technology.

Contract work is not a new concept, whether it's companies offering specialised skills to other companies or individual employees working on contract—but traditionally it has been confined to sectors such as building and engineering. In recent years, this has expanded into almost every industry sector as a result of managers examining ways to improve productivity. In the United States, 13 per cent of the workforce is now on contract work in one form or another and Australia is following a similar pattern.

Contracting arrangements suit energetic, specific-skills people who enjoy project work and find the routine side of many permanent jobs frustrating.

To sell your skills on a freelance basis you need to be a confident, flexible, self-reliant individual:

- you have specific skills and/or technical expertise to offer either as a problem-solver who can add value by improving an organisation's performance or as a temporary employee who takes an existing job over because of illness, maternity leave or staff turnover;
- you know where your skills lie and that there is a market for those skills—no successful track record usually means no work;
- you have experience in handling decision-making on your own—there won't be anyone around to tell you what to do;
- you have an ability to adapt quickly, to understand the workings of the organisation and immediately feel comfortable (remember, you are being paid by the hour so you can't waste time trying to fit in);
- you are a fast learner who understands what the employer expects you to do and what you are supposed to be doing (if you see it's the wrong thing you can't go off on a tangent, because you'll get fired);
- you have an independent outlook—not so independent that you are organisationally intolerant—but where you don't feel a need to belong;

- you have the ability to build relationships—one of the essential requirements of this role is to be able to gain cooperation from people you have no authority over, so it's important to be able to build relationships quickly;
- you have a degree of financial security.

The upside of being a contract executive is usually greater than the downside.

The upside

- You don't get bogged down. If you are working in an organisation where you don't have a rapport with the people, you don't have to live with them forever.
- You have the stimulation of work without the politics or pressures of a full-time commitment.
- You have the freedom to spend more time with your family; more control over your life; and better quality of life.
- You can enjoy the challenge and experience of different environments.
- It can be a stepping stone to permanent work. The organisation has an opportunity to assess you, and you have the opportunity to assess them—before you make a commitment.
- You're hired to achieve an objective and you get immediate feedback and the satisfaction of 'a job well done'. In a full-time job it is often difficult to measure your performance.
- You get a reference every time you finish an assignment. And you can use the old adage: You are only as good as your last job.
- Contracting is a great opportunity to stay in touch with your profession whilst pursuing other avenues.
- Contracting is a great opportunity for mature professional women who want to work, but not from 7 am to 7 pm all year.

The downside

- You can be terminated on the spot for non-performance or for any other reason, such as the project being canned.
- You're not included in all the social interactions within the organisation. You're invisible. Everyone else goes to lunch, or off for Christmas drinks. You generally don't get invited.
- Sometimes cooperation from inside the firm can be difficult because you're going to leave. Why should they put themselves out for you?
- If you're not a quick relationship-builder you could feel isolated, left out, ignored.
- You can be given hack work as well as interesting work. But if it's the former, the upside is that the job is not going to last forever.
- Sometimes you will be bigger than the job and you will have to pursue other avenues for intellectual stimulation.
- Lack of continuity of work. When you are working you are not selling your services, and when you are selling your services you are not earning any money. You can get around this by working through reputable contracting agencies.
- There is a certain amount of financial insecurity.

How do you gauge what you are worth in the marketplace?

A good guide to what you are worth is what you've been paid in the past. Not just what you got in your paycheck but how much it cost the company in real terms. Take into consideration holiday pay, long service leave, superannuation, company car—the total package. If you gauge that on working, say, 2000 hours, then function X might be worth $50.00 per hour. If you only work six months, you may need to load that hourly rate to compensate for the six months you take off.

The contract résumé is based much more on achievement and specific abilities rather than talking about job descriptions. It should be short and succinct, highlighting skills and abilities. It's not about managing people—contract executives are not usually hired to manage other people. (*See* example of a contract résumé on page 227.)

The covering letter focuses on specific skills and specific abilities and solving problems rather than 'I'm the sort of person you should have on your team'. (*See* example of a covering letter on page 226.)

The contract interview

The company is not interested in where you are going in the next five years. Contractors are not hired for their potential. You are hired because you can do the job and you can start tomorrow.

When companies hire contract workers they are making a problem-solving decision rather than a recruitment decision. Personality, style and whether you fit their culture are not usually motivating factors; the prime question for the employer is: Can you achieve the task in this time frame at this cost?

The object of the interview is to focus on what the task is—to get the company to outline the problem and how a solution can be achieved; and to demonstrate how you've handled similar situations in the past.

It is critical to ask the right questions. I can put projects together, review your data-processing systems, put in an accounting package and develop a training program, *but I need to know more about your industry.* What sort of projects are you currently handling where you haven't got anyone to delegate to? What sort of projects do you need to do right now that could make a big impact on your business to help you prosper next year? What do you mean by a documentation person? What do you want it to look like?

The people who make the decisions to take on a contract person are the line managers, not the human resources people (unless they're looking for contract HR people). The line manager will know what the objectives and time frames are, and what the budget is.

To look and sound professional you must look and sound like an expert in your particular field. Your presentation has to be good. The company is buying something (a product) to solve a problem. So that package needs to be right—and that includes dressing to look the part. Your object is to work as many days as you can, so the better your presentation, the more you are going to work.

A contract job can last for a year or more, or one or two days, but the average is sixteen weeks.

Who hires contract executives?

The strongest areas of demand for contract executives are manufacturing, finance and IT, but work can be found in any organisation in the world in need of your specific skills and abilities across a wide range of disciplines.

Contract executives replace absent executives, handle overloads, launch new products, undertake project work and feasibility studies and assume general management responsibilities. They can be computer-literate cost accountants, EDP auditors and treasury accountants, production specialists, quality managers, marketing executives, human resources people and computer project managers—anyone whose skills can be utilised in the marketplace.

People generally find jobs through networking or through a major recruitment organisation which has specialist contracting divisions. There are also a number of agencies which specialise in niche market areas such as accountants, lawyers, doctors, physiotherapists and journalists.

Turnaround management

Turnaround management is another area of contracting where someone is brought in to fill a gap at management level—for example, a line management job, a financial controller, or a position in the human resources area. Or, at a higher level, where a CEO is placed in a company to clean it up, get it back on track and generate profit so it can be packaged for sale.

Management consultancy

Another development of management contracting is the management consultancy area. The traditional approach of a management consultant is to gather the data, analyse it and come up with recommendations as to how the problem should be solved.

However, contract consultants need to have a pragmatic as well as a theoretical approach. They must be able to take the traditional process one step further and follow through to the implementation of their recommendations.

Contract consultants must have hands-on experience. They must be proven performers with a successful track record in their own right and must have experience at the sharp-end of an operation. In addition, they must have the ability to consult, advise and, if necessary, oversee and/or implement their recommendations.

Projects and troubleshooting roles

Where specialised contract executives come into their own is in their ability to either undertake a project or act in a caretaking role while the permanent executive is seconded to a project. Companies take on contract people in these roles to ensure that:

- low permanent staff ceilings are maintained;
- skills are matched to the project in hand;
- a higher level of expertise can be employed for the project than would normally be available;
- permanent staff are able to keep the business operating at full efficiency, ensuring full profitability with negligible disruption.

Generally, management contracting can provide companies with greater expertise and experience, while for you it could be the alternative employment stream you've been searching for.

Here is an example of a covering letter.

STRICTLY PRIVATE AND CONFIDENTIAL

10 April 1999

Mr John Jones
Director
Global Incorporated
1 York Street
SYDNEY NSW 2000

Dear Mr Jones

Please find attached a brief résumé which outlines my particular expertise and achievements in developing marketing strategies for industrial companies. I am now operating as an executive contractor and am available either for short-term or part-time employment on an ongoing consultancy basis.

I believe that in half an hour of your time you would be able to assess my ability to add value and profits to your business.

I will ring you next week to arrange a suitable meeting time.

Yours Sincerely
ROGER SMART

Here is an example of a contract résumé. This is an edited version; in the real version, you would list *all* your relevant employment history.

PRIVATE AND CONFIDENTIAL

PERSONAL DETAILS

Name   Roger Smart

Personal details

          Born 7 March 1968

Education   Bachelor of Applied Science (Computing)

SKILLS AND EXPERIENCE (an edited version)

Industry

- Telecommunications
- Finance
- Education
- Service/Banking
- Manufacturing/Distribution

COMPUTER EXPERTISE

Hardware: IBM PC, Apple Mac, Sun workstation

Operating
systems: Windows NT/95/98, UNIX (Sun, AIX, IRIX,
          System V), VAX VMS, MacOS, MS-DOS

Languages: Visual C++(Active X, COM, MFCs), C/C++,
          Assembly, SQL, FORTRAN, RPL,
          Jave(learning), Visual Basic(learning)

Software
packages: MATLAB, MS-Access, MS-Office,
          Mathematica, Borland-Office, Photoshop,
          Director, Authorware, VisualAge (for Java),
          Visual Studio

Databases: MS-Access, Oracle 7 (learning), SQL 6.5
          (learning), DB2-UDB (learning)

Internet:	Netscape Application Server, Enterprise Server, IIS, Cold-Fusion

Skills

- Systems manager
- Software consultant
- Network performance analyst
- Systems programmer/analyst
- Operations manager

EMPLOYMENT HISTORY

August 1995–

January 1999 *Optus Communications*

Systems Programmer/Analyst (Contract)
Upgraded and maintained real-time software for the Station Management Subsystem and the Remote Monitoring Command and Control system. Designed user interlace, screens and forms. Simulation of hardware and software changes before implementation. Liaised with Engineering and Broadcast Operations Centre on installation and upgrading of station management and control equipment. Diagnosed hardware and software faults on both computer and station management equipment. Operations support for PDP computers.

October 1993–

August 1995 *Flakt Australia Ltd*

Analyst Programmer/Software Consultant (Contract)
Converted accounting system from the PDP 11/44 to the AS/400. Operation and management of PDP and VAX computer systems. Analysed and advised on

performance and security of VAX and PDP.
Designed and wrote sales and invoicing
package to run on PS/2, written in Dataflex.
Analysed and advised on suitable
hardware and software solutions for Flakt
computer network. Hotline support for user
queries on hardware and software.

PART-TIME AND TEMPORARY WORK 2

Part-time work

Part-time work is defined by the Australian Bureau of
Statistics (ABS) as employees who usually work less than 35
hours a week (in all jobs). The changing structure of the
workforce has led to an increase in people working on this
basis. One in four jobs is now part-time.

In the past the downside has often been a low level of
responsibility and boring routine work. However, as management continues to rethink work practices—in one month
37 400 full-time jobs disappeared and 36 600 part-time jobs
were created—the variety and level of part-time work will
create more interesting choices.

For those who want to work on a regular or permanent
basis but with shorter hours, part-time work could be ideal.

Temporary work

Whilst only a low percentage of the Australian workforce,
relative to overseas, is engaged in temporary work, the last
few years have seen a huge increase in organisations requiring

temporary office staff. Temporary work is generally confined to women with secretarial and/or clerical skills, but people with skills in the hospitality, sales and marketing industries, and in telemarketing, are also in demand.

Temporary work is very competitive. Be prepared to take a typing test and prove you are computer literate if you are applying for a keyboard position.

For women returning to the workforce, temporary work is a good way to get your foot back in the door and it can be a stepping-stone to a full-time job. To get a feel for the marketplace, ask for work in a variety of companies.

Various private employment agencies specialise in placing people in these positions. Look under Employment Agencies in the *Yellow Pages* or check the employment section of the newspaper to see who is advertising and the skills they require. Reputable agencies will be members of the Recruitment and Consulting Services (RACS).

A tip for temps: As with contract work, employers are not interested in personality—they want good presentation, good attitude and good skills.

STARTING A SMALL BUSINESS— LOOK BEFORE YOU LEAP

A report on small business in Australia by the Small Business Unit of the Department of Industry, Technology and Commerce found that small and medium-sized enterprises are recognised as:

- contributing more to employment growth than larger firms;
- contributing more than proportionately to innovation

and technology transfer and providing more
opportunities for new ideas and skills to be tested;
- increasingly globalised and internationally competitive as
a result of the adoption of new organisational forms and
new technologies;
- becoming more volatile than the larger firm sectors.

Small business have been estimated to employ more than
56 per cent of the nation's workforce, with more than
2.5 million working in, and/or owning, small businesses.

What is a small business?

According to the traditional view, a small business is any
business of less than 20 employees, except in manufacturing
where 100 is the benchmark; *or* any business with less than
$3 000 000 turnover.

According to the contemporary view, a small business is
any business in which one or two persons only are required
to make all the critical management decisions in areas such
as finance, accounting, personnel, purchasing, marketing,
pricing and strategy.

A sobering fact is that 90 per cent of small businesses fail
within eight years. The reason for this: *bad management!*

What is bad management?

- 10 per cent of failures are due to a lack of industry
experience. In other words, don't open an art gallery if
you can't tell a good painting from a bad one.
- 13 per cent of failures are due to a lack of management
ability. Theoretical knowledge means nothing if you can't
manage events or people.
- 19 per cent of failures are due to a lack of experience
across the board. In a small business you must be an
operator, a salesperson, an administrator and a manager.

If you lack skills in any of these areas you should consider further training or putting your idea on hold.

- 48 per cent of failures are simply due to incompetence— if you haven't demonstrated in the past that you've got what it takes, don't risk your hard-earned capital.

The overriding management error present in the majority of small business failures is *too much borrowed capital*. The higher you gear yourself, the higher the risk and the more effective you have to be at what you do.

Advantages of small business

- Personal satisfaction.
- Independence of decision-making.
- A social role in the community and social recognition.
- Job creation for yourself, perhaps even your children.
- Sense of achievement.
- Opportunity for leadership.
- An effective way to build a capital asset.

Disadvantages of small business

- Risk—it's all yours!
- More bosses than you ever had—the landlord, customers, the government, the garbage collector, your bank manager, suppliers, etc, etc. You're answerable to them all.
- Sole responsibility—no chance to pass the buck.
- Usually longer working days.
- Difficulty taking a holiday—especially in the early years.
- No such thing as time off work because of an imaginary (or real) sickness.
- Fewer people (if any) to share your problems with.
- Often lower wages for a long time.
- Often a large bank debt for a long time.

What will help your small business to succeed?

- Enthusiasm, drive, initiative, self-discipline and commitment.
- Technical/product/specific skills.
- Excellent organisational skills.
- Entrepreneurial ability.
- Health, stamina and personal stability.
- Ability and willingness to listen and learn.
- Proper pricing policies.
- A business plan outlining your (realistic) goals and how you will achieve them.
- Closely monitored cash flow, and realistic projections.
- A healthy respect for profit.
- Determination to succeed.
- Interest on level of borrowings must be affordable from day one. Paying interest on accumulated interest is the beginning of a downhill spiral.

What is profit?

- It is *not* more cash to spend on yourself.
- It is:
  - a test of your performance;
  - a reward for risk taken;
  - a return on your investment;
  - a source of capital for the growth of your business.

Setting up your business

In the preparatory stages talk to your accountant, solicitor, bank manager and business adviser. Most importantly, *do your research* to establish that there is a market for your product/service.

With technology at their fingertips—PCs, paging systems, faxes, answerphones, mobile phones and Internet access—

many people (ABS figures show 4 per cent of the workforce) successfully operate a wide range of businesses from home. However, before you set up your operations they will require careful consideration and research.

There is a small business advisory centre in each State which provides a range of services, including workshops, for aspiring businesspeople. The State Chamber of Commerce also has an advisory service for small business, as does the Australian Chamber of Manufactures. Both require membership to access the service.

The Australian Government Publishing Service (AGPS) has published an excellent series of books devoted to running and managing a small business. They are available through the Commonwealth Government Bookshop in each capital city. Ask for a catalogue.

If you're unemployed you may be able to apply for financial assistance to set up a small business. Your local Centrelink office will be able to advise you.

THE 'PERFECT' NEXT JOB— A PROMPT LIST

Ideal job description

TITLE	Financial Controller
OBJECTIVES	Automatic Processes
IMPACT ON ORGANISATION	Bottom-line savings
AUTHORITY/RESPONSIBILITY	People, assets, budget
	Independence/Autonomy
	How do I want to be managed?
CHALLENGE	I want to build a team
HIGH/LOW RISK	I'm prepared to risk security for higher income
JOB VISIBILITY	Happy with media representation

PROMOTION/GROWTH OPPORTUNITY	Would like to be General Manager in five years
REPORTING RELATIONSHIP	Managing Director
– *direct (line)*	Head of Marketing
– *dotted line (functional)*	Management Support
TRAVEL	Minimum of two overseas trips a year
SALARY RANGE	$55 000 plus
PACKAGE	Must include car and bonus incentives
PERSONAL FACTORS	
– *location*	City
– *length of commute*	Not more than 30 minutes
– *physical surroundings*	Room with a view

Ideal company description

CULTURE/STYLE	I want a company that is structured
SIZE OF COMPANY	$15 million plus turnover
PRODUCT SALES	Margins/direct or indirect/ type of customer
NUMBER OF EMPLOYEES	100+
LOCAL/NATIONAL/ MULTINATIONAL	Pref. local but not critical
PRODUCT/SERVICE	Business to business (not to customers) Not a stagnant industry

RESEARCH STRATEGY

COMPANY   The Giant Lollywater
                        Corporation

CONTACT NAMES   John Smith, Marketing Director

1. Company

PRODUCT/SERVICE   Carbonated Softdrinks/

RANGE   Mineral Water

MARKET SHARE   ⅔rds of national market;
                        small presence in NZ

MARKETING & SALES   Retail outlets only

PLANT AND DISTRIBUTION 1 plant in each State
FACILITIES   producing full range

PRIVATE/PUBLIC OWNERSHIP Public

LOCAL/NATIONAL/   Multinational
MULTINATIONAL

2. Competitors

MAJOR COMPETITORS   Strike Force SofTdrinks

COMPETITIVE   National company pushing for
ADVANTAGES   100% Australian ownership

ACTIVITY RECORD

Week starting: August 16

Networking contract—new

DATE	NAME	COMMENTS
August 16	Rose Coburn	Happy to meet—busy—call back in 10 days
16	John Phillips	Not right person—suggested Tom Wilkins
16	Henry Williams	Happy to meet—Tues. 4 pm August 25
20	Tom Duncan	Busy with merger—doesn't have time!

Networking contracts—follow-up

DATE	NAME	COMMENTS
August 17	Andrew McLeland	Thanks—seeing John next week—keep in touch
17	Elisabeth McCartney	Standard thank you + résumé
20	Geoff Adderley	As above
20	Mary Smith	Send *BRW* article (new job market)
20	Andrew Simmons	Lunch next week
20	Simon Eadie	Thanks, résumé, great meeting with Fiona

Recruitment consultants— advertised positions

DATE	NAME	COMMENTS
August 16	Greg McCartney	Fin. Controller—good fit—send résumé

16	Paul Brisbane	Doesn't advertise jobs—send résumé
16	Warren Baker	Send résumé—100% fit. Interview Tues. 24
20	Kimberley Ingram	Only 35 responses—surprised. Send résumé.
20	Meg Symons	Public sector job—pref. PS experience. Send résumé.

Recruitment consultants—follow-up

DATE	NAME	COMMENTS
August 19	James Anderson	Fortnightly follow-up—couple of things in pipeline
19	Denise Mackay	Fortnightly follow-up
19	Diane Peterson	Ditto
19	Geoff Burns	Ditto
19	Nicki Clarke	Ditto
August 20	Joanna Prior	Received résumé—still sorting—no more info.
20	Elisabeth Woodhew	Apologised didn't get back—follow-up
20	Mark Linkwell	No. 5! Interviewing 4. Follow-up next week.

Direct advertisement response

DATE	NAME	COMMENTS
August 16	Aetna—Phil Went	Send résumé—no further infomation.
16	D.A.S.	Sending job description + criteria (closes Sept. 30).

20	Sony	HR Director wouldn't give name—send résumé
20	DTMS	Good conversation—please! Send résumé. Urgent.

Other activity

DATE	NAME	COMMENTS
August 18		Enrolled Macquarie—Intro PC skills
18	Tim Finnish	Does want survey update—Appt. Aug. 26
18	Small Business Services	No information. Suggested Franchise Association.
PM Aug 18/19/20	McWilliams Foster Home	Building maintenance—3 days next week

ACTIVITY CHART

Week starting: August 16

Time	Mon	Tues	Wed	Thurs	Fri	Sat/Sun
8.00 am	Advert Review plus calls	8.30 Morgans Interview Library	Calls, thank-yous	Recruiter follow-up house painting	TQM breakfast Parra-matta house painting	
12.00 pm	Applicat-ion letters	Net-working meeting Westfield 1.30	Stock Exchange lunch-time talk		Weekly Review	Mum for weekend
3.30 pm	Kids from school	Tech.	Kids from school	Tech. (deadline for OZ politics essay)	Kids from school	
6.00 pm	Squash		Squash			

THINGS TO DO THIS WEEK

Week starting: August 16

A 1. Résumé to Phil Williamson

A 2. Check Charles Sturt closing dates

C 3. Chamber of Manufactures—list of footwear manufacturers

A 4. Call Brian Anders—reconfirm interview Thursday 8.00am

B 5. Arrange for *Financial Review* and *SMH* to be delivered

A 6. Dry-cleaning: green suit, overcoat

C 7. Get copy of latest *EBS* from Sandra

A 8. Return contract to Morgan & Banks

A 9. Buy Saturday's *Newcastle Herald* and *Adelaide Advertiser*

A 10. Cut out ads. from *SMH* and log

B 11. Call Reg at Active for Giant Lollywater Corporation contact

B 12. Get a copy of the above company's annual report

The principles of time management

1. Create a 'to do' list

2. Prioritise tasks using A, B, C
   A = most urgent/important; B = less so; C = not critical

3. As you complete each task, tick it off

TELEPHONE CONTACT LIST

Week starting: August 16

COMPANY	CONTACT & TITLE	TELEPHONE	NOTES
Fisons Pharmaceuticals	Owen Cleal, Human Resources Director	9223 6666	*Bulletin* Article re new product launch
Ajax Chemicals	Tim Atkins Managing Director	9699 9999	Just appointed (*BRW* article 6.4.99)
Morgan & Banks	Andrew Banks CEO	9256 0333	Ask for interview feedback
	John Smith	9777 7777	Does he have a contact at World Inc.?
Smith, Smith, & Smith	John Doe, Financial Controller	9222 2222	Can the company use my expertise with the Brown merger?
Giant Lollywater Corporation	Roger Smart Marketing Manager	9255 5555	Get more information on the soft drinks industry
Small Business Avisory Service		9888 8888	Re Government Assistance
World Conferences		9777 7777	Get more info. on the computer trade show

JOB SEARCH

Tracking sheet

NAME	DATE	COMPANY
Owen Cleal Human Resources Dir.	14 May	Fisons Pharmaceuticals
Tim Atkins MD	14 May	Ajax Chemicals
John Doe	15 May	Smith, Smith, & Smith
Greg McKenzie	15 May	Morgan & Banks
Roger Smart Marketing Manager	18 May	Giant Lollywater Corporation

ADDRESS & PHONE	SPECIFIC POSITION?	RÉSUMÉ SENT	INTERVIEW
4 King St. Adelaide 5000 9223 666	Financial Controller The Aust. 3 May	3 May	17 May
3 Queen St Melbourne 3000 9699 9999	Melbourne *Age* 13 May	16 May	
14 Hunter St Sydney 2000 9222 2222	Poss. contract work	15 May	
Level 11 225 George St Sydney 2000	Financial Controller Ref. GMO2	14 May	21 May
15 Turbine St Brisbane 5000		23 May	

BASIC BUDGETER

TYPE OF EXPENSE		ESTIMATE OF EXPENDITURE			
		Jan	Feb	Mar ...	Annual Total
Housing	Rent				
	Loan or Mortgage Payment				
	Council Rates				
	Electricity				
	Gas/Oil				
	Telephone				
	Maintenance & Repairs				
	Strata Title Fees				
	Furniture				
	TV Rental				
Personal	Clothing & Shoes				
	Hair Care & Cosmetics				
Children	School Fees				
	Clothing				
	Activities and Other				
Food	Supermarket				
	Delicatessen/ Butcher etc.				
	Other				
Transport	Public Transport				
	Taxi				
Financial Securities	Investments				
	Superannuation				
	Building/Contents Insurance				
	Car Insurance				
	Life Insurance				
	Income Protection				
	Medical Insurance				

		Jan	Feb	Mar ...	Annual Total
Motor Vehicle	Registration				
	Licences/Motor Associations				
	Maintenance & Repairs				
	Petrol & Oil				
	Lease/Loan Payments				
Entertainment & Leisure	Restaurants/ Bars				
	Concerts/ Theatre				
	Subscriptions				
	Sports & Fitness				
	Hobbies				
	Holidays				
Health	Pharmacy				
	Doctor				
	Dentist				
	Optometrist				
Miscellaneous	Newspapers & Books				
	Gifts & Donations				
	Other				
	Total Annual Expenses (Add 10% to cover inflation)				

Work	
+ Other	
Total Annual Income	

Total annual income
– Total annual expenses
Annual profit/loss

GLOSSARY OF TERMS AND BUZZWORDS

OUTSOURCING—The farming out of peripheral services to specialist organisations.

COMPETENCIES—The concept of competencies focuses on what is expected of an employee in the workplace rather than on the learning process. It embodies the ability to transfer and apply skills and knowledge to new situations and environments.

KNOWLEDGE WORKER—A term first coined in the 1970s by management guru Peter Drucker to describe the worker of the future. Someone whose knowledge is transportable, who applies to productive work ideas— concepts and information, rather than manual skills.

OUTPLACEMENT PROGRAM: Career Transition Management (CTM)—An employer-assisted career transition course.

PERFORMANCE APPRAISAL—Performance appraisal and review is the technique designed to monitor the performance of individuals and teams in relation to organisation objectives.

TOTAL QUALITY MANAGEMENT (TQM)—A management philosophy that seeks continuous improvement in all processes, products and services of an organisation. It requires a solid customer focus; a preventative approach to quality; a profound understanding of variation; decisions based on measurement; and the creative involvement of employees at all levels.

QUALITY ASSURANCE (QA)—Quality assurance is the ability to provide a formal assurance that goods and services to be supplied have been either assessed as meeting a relevant product standard, or produced by a process assessed as meeting a relevant quality system standard.

LINE FUNCTION—The primary purpose of line function is to be accountable for a measurable monetary impact on the organisation and involves the achievement of objectives through the management of revenue, profit, resources or capital expenditure.

STAFF FUNCTION—The primary purpose of a staff function is providing technical, specialist, strategic or policy advice where determination of a measurable monetary impact is inappropriate or not possible.

PROCESS/PROJECT ORIENTED—Process is continuous and dictated by predictable and measured levels of supply and demand; as opposed to project oriented, which usually has a finite life cycle and is controlled by special requirements.

FURTHER READING

Bolles, R., *What Color is Your Parachute?* Ten Speed Press,
Berkeley, California, USA, 1993.

Covey, S.R., *The 7 Habits of Highly Effective People,*
The Business Library, Australia, 1990.

Davis, M. & Meyer, C., *Blur—the speed of change in the
connected economy*, Ernst & Young, 1998.

Hall, D.T., et al, *The Career is Dead, Long Live the Career*,
Jossey–Bass Inc, 1996.

Medley, H.A., *Sweaty Palms—Revised,* Ten Speed Press,
California, USA, 1992.

Montgomery, B. & Evans, A., *You & Stress,*
Viking O'Neill/Penguin, Australia, 1989.

Scheele, A., *Skills for Success,* Ballantine Books, New York,
USA, 1989.

Scott, D., *Stress That Motivates,* Crisp Publications Inc.,
California, USA, 1992.

Tepper, R., *Power Résumés,* John Wiley & Sons Inc., NY,
USA, 1992.

Zelinski, E.J., *The Joy of Not Working,* Visions International
Publishing, Edmonton, Canada, 1992.

JOB HUNTING?

Save time! Register with Job Hound.

- Job Hound is a proactive service dedicated to 'sniffing out' new job opportunities
- Visit **www.morganbanks.com.au**, *click on* Job Hound, provide a few details, and let Job Hound 'dig' through the jobs on our database and retrieve those which match your preferences

The easy way to create/update your résumé!

- Listen to résumé tips directly from Andrew Banks and Geoff Morgan
- Tailor your résumé for different positions
- Create a professional and easy-to-read resume in electronic or hardcopy format
- Speed up the job application process by sending your résumé electronically to Morgan & Banks
- Visit Résumé Builder at **www.morganbanks.com.au**